market **vegetarian**

market **vegetarian**

easy **organic** recipes
for every occasion

Ross Dobson

photography by Richard Jung

RYLAND
PETERS
& SMALL

LONDON NEW YORK

Dedication

This book is dedicated to all those passionate and hard working local market farmers who provide us with a guarantee of the provenance of our fresh fruit and vegetables.

Design and Photographic Art Direction
Steve Painter
Senior Editor Julia Charles
Production Manager Patricia Harrington
Art Director Leslie Harrington
Publishing Director Alison Starling

Food Stylist Ross Dobson
Prop Stylist Róisín Nield
Indexer Hilary Bird

First published in the United Kingdom
in 2008
by Ryland Peters & Small
20–21 Jockey's Fields
London WC1R 4BW
www.rylandpeters.com

10 9 8 7 6 5 4 3 2

Text © Ross Dobson 2008
Design and photographs
© Ryland Peters & Small 2008

ISBN 978 1 84597 721 4

A catalogue record for this book is available from the British Library.

Printed and bound in China

Notes

• All spoon measurements are level unless otherwise stated.

• Eggs are large unless otherwise specified. Uncooked or partially cooked eggs should not be served to the very old, frail, young children, pregnant women or those with compromised immune systems.

Author's Acknowledgements

It is a privilege to be given the opportunity to create yet another beautiful book with Ryland Peters & Small. Thank you to Alison for your ongoing confidence in me – I look forward to our dinners in London. To Julia, whose editorial queries appear like magic across the vast distance between London and Sydney. Thank you for keeping me on my toes and not missing a trick. Thanks also go to Richard for his beautiful photography – it's always such a pleasure to work with you. And to Steve who always makes such a perfect job of the design. Last, but not least, Róisín whose beautiful props really do make our work so much easier. Thank you all so much.

contents

growers' markets: one degree of separation

In my view good vegetarian cooking is not about reinventing the wheel – the world is already full of wonderful vegetable dishes that I look to for my inspiration. My ethos is to choose quality ingredients, understand the classic flavour combinations and introduce a twist or two to keep things modern and interesting. I should also say that this is not a cookbook exclusively for vegetarians (and it is at this point that I must confess to not being a vegetarian myself). But I am no less discerning about what I choose to buy, cook and eat. I want to be assured that I'm being offered the very best ingredients and it always puts my mind at ease to know where my food has come from.

You may be passionate about the source of your food for ethical or health reasons, or you may just want the freshest and best produce because you enjoy eating well. These days the provenance of what we eat is relevant to everyone and is a highly topical and hotly debated issue. It may seem as if it's only recently that we have become so interested in where our food comes from but for some people it has been a concern for a long time. In parts of the United States the resurgence in fresh food shopping options, such as growers' markets, began in the early 1970s, but it has really only been in the last decade that this movement has gained momentum in other developed countries. There is now a widespread desire to know where our food originates from and many chefs and food writers, myself included, are only too happy to champion the cause.

Today's globalized food market ensures that most of our food can be bought all year round but the obvious problem with buying fruit and vegetables during the months when they do not grow locally is that they have, inevitably, had to travel a considerable distance to reach the shelves of your local supermarket. This means that they have had to be harvested or picked early and before they have had a chance to ripen as nature intended. The ripening process is then stopped in its tracks by refrigerated transport and other forms of high-technology food storage. Not surprisingly, by the time you put the 'fresh' fruit and vegetables in your supermarket trolley they are often lacking in flavour and can be a big disappointment. Market researchers have established that modern consumers like to see the word 'fresh' on food packaging so it's a term that's often used but rarely true. 'Fresh' shelled peas in a plastic tray and covered in shrinkwrapping are already well past their prime – fresh in this case simply means not frozen. You probably won't even see the word fresh used to describe produce on sale at your local growers' or farmers' market; it would be both preaching to the converted and superfluous – of course what's on sale is fresh!

We may think of the concept of a farmers' or growers' market as being a new thing but in many countries around the world the fresh food markets have been a way of life for centuries. I've been lucky enough to see baskets of just-picked, exotic herbs on display at the Aw Taw Kaw markets in Bangkok, daily harvested courgette flowers at the Campo dei Fiori in Rome and squeaky fresh corn-on-the-cob at an Amish stall in Union Square in New York City. True, these are unique and famous marketplaces, and for most of us they are a long way from home, but they are essentially no different to your local market. Whether in the heart of a massive metropolis or the car park of your local school, they all share the same philosophy and purpose. They are a direct link between the grower and the buyer and a place where only one degree of separation exists between you and the origin of your food. The stalls at your local food market are more often than not manned by the growers themselves and they become the guarantors of the provenance of the food you buy there. The weekend is often the only time that they are not in the fields or orchards and for some it's their only day off. Even so, some of the stallholders would have been up since the early hours of the morning gathering, packing and preparing their produce for its short trip to the market – the evidence will be the dirt on their hands. These people are dedicated to growing food with care and concern for the environment and respect for the seasons. This, in turn, has a positive effect on the quality of the food you buy. I do believe that the resulting produce is vastly superior to that which is produced using methods that meet a financial bottom line or grown on a huge, unnatural scale to meet consumer demand.

The other main problem with a globalized market is that it has also gradually and systematically eliminated local producers and in doing so has also diminished many of the unique foods and flavours that were at one time available to us. In being denied a choice of quality produce it seems we have also been alienated from our kitchens. The lack of varieties and types of veggies available at the supermarket has resulted in limited cooking styles, techniques and methods. Supporting your local growers' market will not only have a positive impact on local farm economies but ultimately guarantee the diversity of food available to us over the years to come – surely an investment worth the return. Okay, so the growers' market may not be as convenient as a supermarket. It might be tough to find parking, but you could walk. It might be raining, but you could carry an umbrella. The food might be dirty but this ensures a greater level of intimacy with the food as you have to spend time washing and preparing it yourself. It might only be open one or two days per week but who wants to go shopping more than that anyway? The process is slower and more relaxed. For me, the market becomes a place to escape from the fast pace of modern life and when it comes to food I'm all for slowing things down a little. It's so much fun to go to a local market, meet the growers and talk to them about their produce – in my experience they are only too happy to talk to you and offer advice on what variety of potato or type of mushroom is best suited to your purpose. You may also run into your friends and neighbours so seize the opportunity to have a relaxed chat and even exchange some recipe ideas for all the wonderful things you have just put in your basket. No fluorescent lights, no piped muzak, no trolleys and food encased in plastic. In this fast-paced modern world the marketplace is where we can indulge in a little nostalgia for a more traditional way of life.

The most colourful and exciting stalls at any farmers' market are undoubtedly the fruit and vegetable ones. They are a theatre of colour and every few weeks, as the curtain closes on one class act it opens on another. We drift through the fresh, green days of early spring, when pickings are relatively slim, but we have shoots and stems such as asparagus and forced rhubarb to keep us entertained. We gradually see the arrival of the peas, beans and pods of late spring and then the jewel-like vine fruits of summer, including my personal favourite, the tomato. Tender summer squashes and leafy salad vegetables are gradually replaced on the stalls by early autumn produce in hues that define autumn; deep purple aubergines, blood-red plums, rust-coloured pumpkins and butternut squash. And so it continues throughout the year – plentiful, organically grown, seasonal food, at its best.

In developing the recipes for this book I focused on what I feel like eating at different times of the week or on different occasions. I like nothing better than enjoying a bottle of wine and sharing a plate of food with friends so I've included a selection of my favourite little dishes, dips and parcels – all just right for grazing and relaxed entertaining. On weekdays I want to eat well but I don't want to spend too long getting my food ready because of other demands on my time. What is needed is good food fast – some tomatoes warmed in a little olive oil, their sweetness offset with a handful of bitter radicchio, and tossed through my favourite pasta – basically midweek meals that are easier done than said! It is on Saturdays that I am truly inspired. For many of us folks dedicated to buying our produce locally, this is market day. I stock up on great, truly fresh ingredients in the morning and have the rest of the day free to spend in my kitchen. I find it a comforting, meditative place to be and my idea of heaven is being enveloped in the aroma of freshly-baked pumpkin soda bread as I experiment, creating new dishes with all the goodies I've procured that day. Some ingredients lend themselves to simply being thrown into a pot with a few herbs (the alchemy of one-pot cooking) so I've devoted a chapter to soups and stews. I also have a sweet tooth so could not resist including some treats but they are all developed around seasonal fruits so you need not feel too guilty – you can quite literally have your cake and eat it!

know your onions: buying market produce

Here you'll find some useful tips on what to look for when out shopping and how to store your produce to keep it at its best. I find it easier to categorize vegetables and fruit by how I use them in the kitchen rather than strictly by their botanical family, so that's what I've done here.

root vegetables and winter squashes

potato sweet potato celeriac parsnip turnip swede carrot beetroot pumpkin squash

These are the dirty boys of the market – the vegetables that grow close to or underneath the ground. They are generally most abundant and at their peak during the cooler months.

Arguably the most popular is the humble **potato**. Hailing originally from South America, it was introduced to Europe by the early explorers of the New World. There are more than 400 varieties in existence, though most of these are not widely available. They come in so many shapes, colours and sizes that buying what you need can be confusing. To simplify matters, there are really only two main types of potato – waxy and floury. Waxy potatoes tend to be young, new potatoes. They are less starchy and stay firm making their flesh best for recipes where you want your potato to hold its shape such as the Taleggio and Potato Tortilla (see page 35). Floury potatoes, usually maincrop, are more starchy so they bake, roast, mash and fry well – perfect for Crispy Oven Wedges (see page 22). When buying any sort of potato avoid any that seem withered, have damp patches or are sprouting. New potatoes should ideally be eaten within 2–3 days but maincrop potatoes will keep for several months in a dark, cool, dry place. **Sweet potatoes** have a distinctive sugary flavour and are excellent baked, mashed, roasted or used in soups such as my Sweet Potato and Coconut Soup (see page 79). When buying sweet potatoes do choose small ones as the larger ones can be rather fibrous. They will keep in a dark, cool, dry place for about 8 days. **Celeriac** is actually the root of a variety of celery and has a similar, though milder, flavour. When grated and eaten raw it's crunchy but when cooked its texture is more like potato. Choose firm and smooth vegetables, still with their tops on, which should be fresh and lively looking. They will keep for a few days in a dark, cool place. **Parsnips** were widely used throughout the Middle Ages before the potato had been introduced. They are related to carrots and similarly sweet and delicious – try the Roasted Parsnip and Garlic Dip (see page 18). Choose small or medium-sized ones that feel firm and don't have any sprouting roots. **Turnips** and **swedes** are close relatives as both belong to the cabbage family. Turnips have a distinctive peppery flavour, while swedes are more earthy and sweeter. Buy the youngest, smallest ones you can find, ideally with fresh green tops. The orange **carrots** we know and love today originally came from Holland, but up until the Middle Ages all carrots were purple! Growers often delight in such oddities and you might be lucky enough to find some at your local farmers' market. All vegetables have a better flavour if they are grown organically, but this is particularly true of carrots. Look for bunches of young, tapered, pencil-thin ones that still have their feathery tops attached. For a real treat bake the Carrot and Walnut Cake on page 146. Glorious **beetroots** have been eaten since Roman times. Delicious when roasted, boiled or simply sliced into wedges and added to salads – see my Home-made Cheese with Roasted Baby Beetroot, Fennel and Pine Nuts on page 106. Always buy small baby beetroots which have their whiskers intact and at least 5 cm of leaf stalk at the top; if they are too closely cropped they will bleed during cooking. They will keep for several weeks in a cool place. **Winter squashes** lend themselves to the same cooking styles and flavourings as root veggies so I've included them here. There are a huge number of varieties and to add to the confusion, many are known by several different names. The most famous is of course **pumpkin** with its sweet, slightly honeyed flavour that works perfectly in my Orange Vegetable and Spring Onion Pilau (see page 75). Other popular squashes include the pear-shaped **butternut**, a reliable everyday variety that will work in pretty much any recipe that calls for squash. Try the Spaghetti with Butternut Squash, Sage and Pecorino on page 60. Try to buy them firm and unblemished with smooth skins. All winter squashes can be stored for long periods in a cool place.

green vegetables

spinach swiss chard cauliflower broccoli savoy cabbage spring greens kale pak-choi

Greens of one sort or another are available throughout the year. It seems that whenever one finishes, another one comes into season.

Spinach is arguably the most versatile of all the green veggies. Almost every cuisine around the world features it in some form or other from Italy to the Middle East. I like to cook a nutritious Baked Spinach Mornay (see page 122) as a brunch dish. It grows all year round and you'll have no difficulty buying it fresh so don't settle for tired or floppy stalks. It will keep in the fridge for 1–2 days.

Swiss chard is similar to spinach but has bigger leaves and a stronger flavour – I use it to make a Swiss Chard, Feta Cheese and Egg Pie (see page 126). Avoid buying any with withered leaves or flabby stems. Store in a cool place and eat within 3–4 days. **Cauliflower** was introduced to Europe by the Moors who took it to Spain but it's thought to have come originally from China. I'm a big fan and keen to show how delicious it can be when it's cooked well – do try my Spiced Cauliflower with Red Pepper and Peas (see page 79) or Cauliflower and Caper Berries on Halloumi (see page 32). When choosing your cauliflower look out for a creamy white and unblemished head with outer leaves that curl tightly around it. Store it in a cool place for no longer than 1–2 days. **Broccoli** is a relatively modern vegetable. It was developed in Italy from the now trendy purple sprouting broccoli. There is actually little to choose between them in taste so it's just a question of whether you prefer the compactness of a head or the leafiness of the sprouting variety. When buying it choose loose bundles, rather than pre-wrapped ones. It should be firm and make a cracking sound when the florets are snapped from the stem. Avoid any that look wilted or have damaged flowerheads. A head of broccoli will keep in the fridge for 2–3 days. Check out my Spaghetti with Broccoli, Walnuts and Ricotta on page 53. There are many varieties of cabbage but all share the same unfortunate problem of a rank smell and flavour if overcooked so the trick is not to overcook them! **Savoy cabbage**, with its crimped or curly leaves has a mild flavour and is particularly tender, hence its popularity. **Spring greens** have loose heads and a pale, yellow-green heart – they are only available in spring and delicious simply steamed and served with butter. Dark and leafy **kale** and **curly kale** are not cabbages but a variety of brassica (as is the Chinese green **pak-choi**) and have a minerally taste, similar to broccoli, that I love. Avoid buying cabbages or greens that look or feel puffy and they should keep in a cool place for several days.

leaves – perfect for the Old-fashioned Garden Salad on page 43. Crispheads, such as **iceberg**, have a nice crunch but not such a great flavour. Looseheads are non-hearting lettuces with loose leaves and these include **lollo rosso** and **oakleaf**. They don't have the best flavour but do look fantastic in your salad bowl! **Cos** (or Romaine) lettuce comes originally from the Greek islands where it was found by the Romans. It is generally considered to be the most delicious lettuce because of its firm texture and faintly nutty and sweet flavour. It's the must-have ingredient for an authentic Caesar salad. As well as lettuce there are a number of other salad leaves – **rocket** being the trendiest. Its hot, peppery taste adds a flavour kick to any salad. **Watercress** is probably the most pungent of all the salad leaves and has a distinctly raw flavour. Just a few sprigs will perk up a mixture of milder-tasting leaves and it makes a deliciously peppery soup (see Watercress and Pea Soup on page 96). **Chicory** (also known as Belgian or French endive and witlof), **radicchio**, **endive** and **escarole** are close relatives and share a similar taste. Chicory can be eaten raw but are often baked, stir-fried or poached. Radicchio looks like a small head of lettuce and is the painted lady of the salad leaf world with its deep wine-red leaves and striking cream ribs. Again it can be eaten raw or as a hot vegetable but does lose it's gorgeous colour when cooked. Curly endive, more commonly known as **frisée** looks pretty and delicate because of its frilly leaves but actually has a rather bitter taste so is better mixed with milder salad leaves. At farmers' markets leaves are often sold in bags or bunches or even buckets and barrels so that you can help yourself. Do look out for mesclun (from the French mescla meaning 'to mix') a nifty salad mix of assorted small young leaves which often includes oakleaf, radicchio, frisée, baby spinach and rocket. The leaves can be simply tossed in a light, lemony dressing or a mustardy vinaigrette. Avoid buying any leafy salad vegetables that are limp, wilted or shiny. Keep round lettuces wrapped in dampened kitchen paper in the fridge. Wash loose leaves in water (do not soak) and dry them very well. Store them in the fridge in a clean, sealed plastic bag.

leafy salad vegetables
iceberg lollo rosso oakleaf cos rocket
watercress chicory radicchio endive
escarole frisée

Salad leaves are hugely popular today and there are plenty to choose from. Some are lettuces, while others belong to vegetable families – what they have in common is that they are eaten raw and often what we crave in the warmer summer months.

Round lettuces are sold in heads. Butterheads are the classic 'Peter Rabbit' kitchen garden lettuces with floppy loosely packed

peas, beans and pods
garden peas broad beans green beans
sweetcorn

Probably the first vegetables to be cultivated by man, peas and beans have been found in settlements from the late Stone Age onwards. They were valuable to ancient man as they could be dried and stored, which meant that food was available all year round.

Garden peas are one of the delights of summer and are best when absolutely fresh. So, many 'fresh' peas you see wrapped in plastic at the supermarket are already past their best. Buy them still in their

pods from a grower and enjoy them as soon as possible. **Broad beans** are one of man's earliest foods. They grow in most climates and soils and were a staple food throughout the Dark Ages and Middle Ages and only replaced by the potato in the 17th and 18th centuries. As with peas, try to buy broad beans are fresh as possible and eat them as soon as you can. Pods should be small and tender and the beans nutty and sweet with skins that don't need to be removed. **Green beans**, also known as French beans belong to the same large and varied family as Thai beans and yellow wax beans. They are widely used in France and an essential ingredient in my Niçoise-style Brown Rice Salad on page 40. Beans should be bright and crisp. Avoid wilted ones, or those with overly mature pods which feel spongy when lightly squeezed. Green beans do not keep well so use as soon as possible after buying or picking them. Similarly, as soon as **sweetcorn** is picked, its sugar begins to turn to starch. The flavour fades and the kernels toughen so the quicker it goes from crop to pot the better! Look for husks that are clean and green with tassles which are golden with no sign of matting. The corn itself should look plump and yellow. Don't keep husks too long – a day at most in the fridge. Try one of my recipes that's designed to showcase fresh sweetcorn at its best – Summer Sweetcorn Soup on page 66 or Sweetcorn Relish on page 36.

vegetable fruits and summer squashes

tomatoes peppers chillies aubergines courgettes

The 'fruits' of the vegetable world are the most colourful, and most versatile, of all veggies. They are widely used throughout the world to add jewel-like colour, flavour and texture to all kinds of recipes.

Along with onions, **tomatoes** are arguably the most important fresh ingredient used in any kitchen, especially in the Mediterranean where they are absolutely essential. Used with garlic and olive oil, they create the basis of so many dishes that it's hard to find any in which they are not included! There are a staggering 7,000 varieties, ranging from beefsteak to cherry, and they range in colour from bright red to vibrant yellow. Sadly many of these varieties are new hybrids, specially developed to be available all year round. I'm not a fan and have long lamented the availability of the bland year-round tomato, so it's good to see a resurgence in popularity of what I call 'real' tomatoes that have been grown outdoors, on a vine planted in soil and in the sunshine. When buying tomatoes first use your eyes then your nose. Overripe tomatoes will smell a bit rancid, don't buy any that smell less than wonderful. Choose fruits that are firm and don't worry if they are underripe. In summer either keep them in a

bowl or line them up on a sun-drenched windowsill to ripen but do not store them in the fridge. The hybrid varieties never seem to ripen or for that matter go off which just can't be a good thing! **Peppers** and **chillies** are both members of the capsicum family. From a culinary point of view the only difference between them is their heat – chillies are hot and pungent and peppers are sweet and mild. Both can be eaten raw, stir-fried, grilled or roasted and their shape makes them perfect for stuffing. Peppers are available in a range of colours, from green (the least mature with a fresh 'raw' flavour) to red peppers which are ripened green peppers and much sweeter. When you buy peppers or chillies they should be glossy and firm – avoid any that look dull and wrinkled. They will keep for a few days in the fridge. I think the versatility of the **aubergine** is unsurpassed – they are grown and cooked all over the world and feature in a multitude of dishes. They are many varieties, according to their country of origin, ranging from cute little pea aubergines in Thailand to the glossy, dark purple zeppelin-shaped ones grown in the West. All have a similar bland yet smoky flavour and a flesh that is spongy when raw, but soft after cooking (see page 85 for my Aubergine, Tomato and Red Lentil Curry). When buying aubergines choose ones that feel heavy and quite firm to the touch and have glossy, clear skins. They will keep well in the fridge for up to 2 weeks. **Courgettes** are the best-loved summer squash. They are quick to cook and tender with a delicate flavour. They should always be firm and glossy – avoid any that feel squashy or look limp. Choose small, young ones for the best flavour and if they still have their flowers attached so much the better as they are delicious to eat – see the Baked Courgette Flowers on page 89.

shoots and stems

asparagus fennel celery artichoke

Vegetables in which the whole or part of the stalk is eaten are classified as shoots or stems. Some, like asparagus, are early season vegetables, others, such as the globe artichoke arrive later in the warmer summer months.

Unless you are lucky enough to grow your own **asparagus** it's definitely a luxury. Its price, even in season, sets it apart from other vegetables. The spears have an intensely savoury flavour that's perfect with eggs (see Asparagus, Sweetcorn and Goats' Cheese Frittata on page 56) or pasta. Asparagus has a relatively short growing season from late spring to early summer. When buying asparagus the tips should be slightly furled and the stalks fresh and straight. It will keep for several days. It's best to untie the bundles and stand them in a jug of cold water in the fridge. **Fennel** is hugely popular in Italy where it is used raw, simply sliced into salads (see page 26) or oven-baked until tender. It has a pleasing aniseed flavour and the feathery fronds can be used like a herb to add flavour towards the end of cooking or as a garnish. Buy small tender bulbs. They should be clean and white with no bruises and the fronds should be green and lively. It will keep for a day or 2 in the fridge. **Celery** has also been added to salads for centuries for its sharp, distinctive flavour and crunchy texture. If possible buy unwashed white celery. It might look 'dirty' but it has a better flavour than the pristine but rather bland green variety. Look for fresh-looking leaves and straight stems. It will keep for several days in the fridge but if limp it can be revived by wrapping it in kitchen paper and standing it in a jug of water as you would cut flowers. **Globe artichokes** are synonymous with summer and, like the heads of cauliflower and broccoli, they are the flower of an edible plant, in this case a thistle. Chargrilled as an antipasti, tossed into pasta or whizzed up in a soup (such as the Globe Artichoke, Tarragon and Roquefort soup on page 103) these photogenic vegetables are always a treat. At their best artichokes should be fresh, crisp, with a bloom on their leaves and the inner leaves wrapped tightly round the choke. They will keep for 2–3 days in the fridge but should be eaten as soon as possible after buying them.

pungent bulbs

onions shallots leeks garlic chives

Known as alliums, there are more than 300 distinct species in the onion family but only a handful are used for culinary purposes. Although there are some wild forms, most are cultivated but the one thing they all have in common is their pungent smell and flavour.

Alongside tomatoes, **onions** are almost certainly the most important ingredient in the kitchen. They can be used raw in salads, browned to give depth of flavour in a stew or gently fried until soft and caramelized for a savoury tart. Try both the Crispy Onion Rings on page 21 or the Slow-cooked Onion and Cider Soup on page 69 and you'll see just just how versatile they are! Onions will keep well stored in a cool, dry place but don't store them in the fridge as they will go soft. Spring onions are simply early-maturing varieties of onion. They have a mild, sweet flavour with a fresh, green snap, which makes them good in salads, Asian-style stir-fries or used as a tasty garnish, as I've done with the Vegetable Potstickers with Orange Dipping Sauce on page 25. Unlike older onions they do not store well but can be kept for a few days in a cool place or the fridge but are best used really fresh. **Shallots** are distinct from onions as they grow in clusters of bulbs. They are also smaller and have finer layers as they contain less water. Shallots can be used much in the same way as onions but they are milder so are good for dishes where you want a more subtle flavour. They should be firm without any green shoots and will keep well for several months in a

cool, dry place. **Leeks** have their own distinct flavour but are, again, a versatile ingredient. They are wonderful in soups and broths, pies and casseroles or simply braised. There are many varieties but little to choose between them in terms of flavour. They can range in size from tiny baby leeks that can be steamed whole as you would asparagus or larger tougher ones that need more cooking. Always buy crisp, firm leeks with perky green parts. **Garlic** is an ingredient few modern cooks, including me, would be without. It was at one time known rather unfairly as 'stinking rose' and in Victorian times considered offensive and acrid. In today's kitchen its uses are infinite – softened in butter or oil as a base for risottos, pasta sauces, stews, soups, casseroles and curries; roughly chopped and sizzled in hot oil for a few seconds in a stir-fry; or finely minced and used in a salad dressing. As a general rule the smaller the bulb, the stronger the flavour. Fresh, new-season garlic has a subtle, mild flavour so it's particularly good if you are using it raw. Garlic bulbs should be firm and round with clear, papery skins. Avoid any that are beginning to sprout. They are best stored in a cool, dry place as damp air will turn the cloves to a grey powder. The aromatic stems of **chives** are used raw to add a faint onion flavour. Sprinkle them over egg dishes, soups or pasta, or stir through sour cream or soft cheese to give it bite. Buy them green and firm, not too floppy and store them in the fridge for just a few days.

mushrooms

field cep morel chanterelle white chestnut oyster portobello enokitake shiitake

You will often find a stall at the market specializing in mushrooms as there are so many edible varieties, both wild and cultivated.

Wild mushrooms are usually more expensive as they are seasonal and gathered by foragers. The most readily available are the wide and flat **field** mushrooms which are perfect for stuffing and baking (see Baked Mushrooms with Manchego Béchamel on page 26). Other more exclusive wild varieties you will see include **cep**, **morel** and **chanterelle**. All make an indulgent addition to soups and stews and are delicious with pasta (see Wild Mushroom Lasagne on page 129). Cultivated varieties include **white** (the very young ones are best known as button mushrooms), **chestnut**, **oyster** and the giant **portobello** which are delicious with pasta (see recipe on page 100). These are widely available most of the year as they are grown in subterranean conditions and thus unaffected by the seasons. Some Asian varieties are now cultivated including the cute little Japanese **enokitake** and popular **shiitake**. All fresh mushrooms should be kept in paper bags and stored in the fridge. Plastic bags or punnets will make them sweat and eventually they turn slippery and unappetizing. It's always best to eat them within 2–3 days.

summer stone fruits

peaches nectarines apricots plums cherries

These delicious fruits all grow on trees in summer and are soft and juicy with a single, central stone. **Peaches** are sometimes known as 'the queen of fruits' and it's not hard to see why. To me they are the perfect fresh fruit for eating raw. Their fuzz-free cousins **nectarines** are also deliciously moreish. All stone fruits, especially **plums** and **apricots** respond well to being gently poached (see Coconut Creamed Rice with Poached Plums on page 152) and also work well in cakes as their juiciness keeps things moist (try the Upside-down Peach Cake on page 143). Unfortunately they don't travel well so try to buy stone fruit as near to where it has grown as possible. Once they are picked they will soften at room temperature but not ripen. Look for fruit at the market that smells ripe and gives slightly when gently pressed. All can be refrigerated in a paper bag for a few days. **Cherries** are one of the great delights of summer. Choose plump ones with shiny, unblemished skins. It's best to buy them still on the stalk which should be green and flexible, not dry and brown. Unwashed cherries will keep for a few days if refrigerated; it's best to wash them just before serving.

autumn orchard fruit

apples pears

The most popular of all fruits, **apples** are good eaten raw but also perfect for baking. The number of varieties is enough to make your head spin so it's best to keep it simple and ask your supplier to recommend something suitable for your purpose. They are divided into two groups – dessert apples (such as Braeburn, Cox's Orange Pippin and Egremont Russet) which are good for munching on as a healthy snack, and tarter cooking apples (such as Bramley's and Blenheim Orange) that are best for sauces, pies and tarts. Apples continue to ripen after being picked and if left too long they become mealy, floury and unappetizing. Try to find just-picked fruit at the market with stalks intact and dry and taut skin. Don't be seduced by the colour of an apple's skin – thick, brilliant red, waxy skins often have woolly, tasteless flesh. Apples can be stored in the fridge or in a dark, cool, dry place. There are now almost as many varieties of **pears** as there are apples. (Try the Salad of Winter Fruit on page 43). They are more fragile than apples and deteriorate very quickly, becoming squashy and unpleasant. Test for ripeness by pressing gently; the fruit should give a little, but still be quite firm. Ripe pears can be stored in the fridge for a few days and unripened ones should be kept in a bowl at room temperature, where they will ripen in 2–3 days.

soft berries

strawberries raspberries blackberries

Whether wild or cultivated, fresh berries are always a treat and the best-flavoured **strawberries** are sweet summer ones. There is something satisfying about foraging for your own berries so if you have the chance to do so give it a try. Sweetly intense **raspberries** are in fact a member of the rose family, as are **blackberries**, and, as such, are both more fragile than strawberries. It's best not to wash them as it ruins their texture. When buying any berries check that those at the bottom of the punnet are not damaged or mouldy. Ideally berries should be eaten the day they are picked or bought but they will keep in the fridge, loosely covered, for not longer than 2 days. Remove from the fridge at least an hour before eating.

citrus fruits

lemons limes oranges

Citrus fruits are packed with juice and have a tough, bitter peel that contains aromatic oils. **Lemons** are always associated with Mediterranean-style cooking as they are one of the key flavourings used and are a kitchen essential for me. **Limes** have thinner, smoother skins and are also highly aromatic. Unlike lemons they grown in tropical regions and are an essential ingredient in South-east Asian and Mexican cooking. **Oranges** are also valued for their fragrant zest and their blossoms. When buying any citrus fruit choose unwaxed, unblemished and firm fruits that feel heavy for their size as this tells you that they will be juicy. Mould forms quickly on all citrus fruit so keep them in a dry place; a fruit bowl is fine for a few days but in humid conditions keep them in the fridge and they should keep for up to 2 weeks.

rhubarb

Strictly speaking **rhubarb** is not a fruit, but a vegetable. It is too sour to eat raw but has a distinctive and delicious flavour when cooked and sweetened and is in its element when served with custard (see the Rhubarb and Custard Pots on page 140). Early forced rhubarb is vivid pink, tender and a real treat, so keep your eyes out for that at the market and by buying it you will probably be supporting a local industry. Later maincrop rhubarb is more tart but it's ideal for baking in a cake or crumble. When buying rhubarb go for crisp, firm and bright stalks that release sap when you snap them. It can be stored for a few days in the fridge.

sharing plates

trio of vegetable dips with spelt toasts

Have you ever been lucky enough to share a plate of mixed dips at a Turkish restaurant? It's the vibrant colours that first grab my attention, quickly followed by the delicious flavours. These dips are all made with root vegetables, including the ubiquitous carrot, all too often lurking at the bottom of your veggie box. They all have a creamy texture, so the crisp spelt toasts make a nice nutty contrast.

roasted parsnip and garlic dip

25 g chilled butter, cubed
90 ml double cream
½ teaspoon sea salt
¼ teaspoon white pepper
500 g parsnips, peeled and sliced
1 garlic bulb, cut in half

Serves 6–8

Preheat the oven to 180°C (350°F) Gas 4. Lightly butter a small baking dish. Put the cream in a small bowl and stir in the salt and pepper.

Put the parsnips in the baking dish with the garlic. Pour the cream over the top, cover with foil and cook in the preheated oven for 45 minutes. Remove the garlic and let cool. When cool enough to handle, squeeze the soft, baked garlic directly into the bowl of a food processor or blender and discard the skin. Add the remaining ingredients and process until smooth. Transfer to a serving dish and cover until ready to serve.

beetroot and caraway dip

3 medium beetroots, uncooked
1 tablespoon prepared horseradish sauce
90 g sour cream
1 teaspoon caraway seeds
sea salt and white pepper

Serves 6–8

Put the beetroots in a large saucepan and cover with cold water. Bring to the boil and let boil for about 45–50 minutes, topping up the water from time to time as necessary. They are ready when a skewer goes through them with little resistance. Drain and let cool. When cool enough to handle, peel and discard the skins. Roughly chop and put in a food processor or blender with the other ingredients and process until smooth. Transfer to a serving dish and cover until ready to serve.

spiced carrot dip

250 ml vegetable stock
4 medium carrots, chopped
2 tablespoons light olive oil
1 small red onion, chopped
2 garlic cloves, chopped
1 large red chilli, chopped
1 teaspoon fenugreek seeds
1 teaspoon ground cumin
sea salt and white pepper

Serves 6–8

Put the stock in a saucepan and add the carrots, oil, onion and garlic. Bring to the boil, then reduce the heat to low and simmer for 15–20 minutes, until almost all the liquid has evaporated and the carrots are soft. Add the chilli, fenugreek and cumin and stir-fry for 2–3 minutes. Transfer the mixture to a food processor or blender and whizz until blended but still with a rough texture. Season to taste, transfer to a serving dish and cover until ready to serve.

spelt toasts

100 g spelt
1 tablespoon dried yeast
250 g spelt flour
½ teaspoon sea salt
plain flour, for dusting

Makes about 40 toasts

Put the spelt in a sieve and rinse well under cold running water. Put it in a saucepan with 1 litre water and bring to the boil. Reduce the heat to low, cover with a lid and cook for 45 minutes. Remove the lid and boil rapidly until almost all the liquid has evaporated. Meanwhile, put the yeast in a small bowl with 4 tablespoons warm water, stir, cover and let rest in a warm place until the mixture is frothy. While it is still warm, put the spelt in a bowl with the spelt flour, salt, 125 ml tepid water and the yeast and stir to bring the mixture together to form a sticky dough. Put the dough on a lightly floured work surface and gently knead for 1 minute. Carefully transfer the dough to a lightly oiled bowl, cover with a tea towel and let rise in a warm place for about 1–1¼ hours, until it has risen and doubled in size.

Preheat the oven to 200°C (400°F) Gas 6. Tip the dough out onto a lightly oiled baking tray and, using floured hands, form the dough into a loaf about 20 x 10 cm, tapering at the ends. Bake the bread in the preheated oven for 40 minutes. Carefully slide the loaf off the tray and directly onto the oven shelf, then bake for a further 5 minutes. Remove from the oven and let cool. To serve, slice into ½-cm wide pieces and toast under a hot grill until golden and crispy on both sides.

crispy onion rings with Parmesan aioli

These are a good thing to cook at the same time as the croquettes, especially if, like me, you don't cook fried food often. You don't have to be too fussy and cook one ring at a time – they taste just as delicious cooked in clumps. Enjoy them warm with the aioli as a dip.

2 red onions, sliced into ½-cm thick rings
2 white onions, sliced into ½-cm thick rings
250 ml buttermilk (or 250 ml full-fat milk combined with 1 tablespoon lemon juice)
55 g chickpea flour (such as Indian besan)
60 g cornflour
1 teaspoon sea salt
2 eggs
500 ml vegetable oil

Parmesan aioli:
2 egg yolks
2 garlic cloves, crushed
2 teaspoons freshly squeezed lemon juice
200 ml light olive oil
25 g Parmesan cheese, finely grated
sea salt and white pepper

Serves 4

To make the aioli, put the egg yolks, garlic and lemon juice in a small bowl and whisk until just combined. Whisk constantly as you add the oil, very slowly at first but building up to a steady stream. Stir in the Parmesan and season with salt and pepper. Set aside.

Put the onion slices in a large bowl and gently toss to separate the rings. Add the buttermilk and stir. Set aside for 1 hour. Put the chickpea flour, cornflour and salt in a bowl. Make a small well in the centre. Use a slotted spoon to remove the onions from the buttermilk (reserving the buttermilk) and transfer them to a colander to drain off any excess liquid. Put 125 ml of the reserved buttermilk in a bowl and beat in the eggs until just combined. Pour this mixture into the flour mixture and beat well with a wooden spoon to form a smooth, thick batter.

Put the oil in a frying pan set over medium/high heat. Toss a handful of onion rings into the batter and lift them out with a slotted spoon (letting any excess batter drip back into the bowl). Put them in the frying pan. Cook for about 1 minute, or until golden. Remove from the oil with a slotted spoon and drain on kitchen paper. Repeat with the remaining onion rings. Serve warm with the Parmesan aioli.

potato and parsnip croquettes

Some form of fried potato croquette turns up in almost all styles of cuisine including German, Dutch, Spanish and the delicious alloo ki tiki from India. I guess they must be so popular because of the harmonious pairing of potatoes, salt and hot oil. I like to use a floury potato for these croquettes, such as Desirée, as it fluffs up nicely when boiled and mashed. The parsnip adds an interesting flavour dimension, as it is a little bitter and sweet at the same time.

500 g potatoes, peeled and quartered
1 parsnip, peeled and quartered
25 g butter, plus 1 tablespoon for frying
2 tablespoons finely chopped parsley
2 eggs
100 g dry breadcrumbs from a day-old loaf of bread
2 tablespoons plain flour, for dusting
vegetable oil, for shallow-frying
sea salt and freshly ground black pepper
sweet German mustard, to serve

Makes 18 croquettes

Put the potatoes and parsnip in a large saucepan and cover with boiling water. Set over high heat and boil for 12–15 minutes until tender. Drain and return to the warm pan. Add the 25 g butter and mash well until the mixture is lump-free. Stir in the parsley and season well with salt and pepper. Cover and refrigerate until the mixture is completely chilled.

Break the eggs into a bowl and beat well to combine. Put the breadcrumbs in a separate bowl. Lightly flour your hands and work surface. Take 1 heaped tablespoon of mixture and form it into a small sausage, tapping the ends on the floured work surface so that they are flattened rather than tapered. Dip the croquette in the beaten egg, then roll it in the crumbs until coated. Put on a baking tray lined with baking paper. Repeat until all of the potato mixture has been used and refrigerate until ready to cook.

Put the 1 tablespoon butter in a frying pan and pour in sufficient oil to come halfway up the sides of the pan. Heat the pan over medium heat until the butter begins to sizzle. To test if the oil is hot enough, sprinkle a few crumbs into it – they should sizzle on contact. Cook the croquettes in batches for 2–3 minutes, turning often, until golden and crisp all over. Remove from the oil using a slotted spoon and drain on kitchen paper to remove excess oil. Serve warm with the mustard on the side.

When was the last time you stirred some freshly made pesto into a big bowl of hot spaghetti? It's an aromatic and heady experience. Food manufacturers like us to believe that pesto keeps in a jar or plastic tub in the fridge, but I couldn't disagree more. It soon oxidizes, turning bitter, brown and oily, and quickly becomes a lesser version of its glorious former self. This vibrant pesto made with handfuls of garden-fresh basil and parsley will knock your socks off and surpass anything you can buy in supermarkets.

crispy oven wedges with homemade pesto sauce

2 large, floury potatoes (such as Desirée), each cut into 8–10 wedges
2 tablespoons light olive oil

pesto sauce:
2 handfuls of fresh basil leaves
1 handful of fresh flat leaf parsley leaves
1 garlic clove, chopped
1 tablespoon freshly squeezed lemon juice
50 g pine nuts, lightly toasted
65 ml light olive oil
50 g Parmesan cheese, finely grated

Serves 4

To make the pesto, put the basil, parsley, garlic, lemon juice and pine nuts in a food processor and process until finely chopped. With the motor of the food processor running, add the oil in a steady stream until it is all incorporated, then transfer the mixture to a bowl and stir in the Parmesan. Cover and set aside until you are ready to serve.

Bring a large saucepan of water to the boil and add the potatoes. Boil them for 5 minutes, then drain and let cool completely.

Preheat the oven to 220°C (425°F) Gas 7. Drizzle the oil onto a large roasting tray and put in the oven for 5 minutes to heat up. Arrange the potatoes on the tray in a single layer and cook in the preheated oven for about 8 minutes, until they are golden on the underside. Turn them over and cook for another 8 minutes, until crisp and golden all over.

Transfer the hot wedges to a plate and serve with the pesto on the side to use as a dip.

Modern Spanish tapas bars are very popular just now. I hope it's not just a passing trend and that they are here to stay, as tapas dishes are casual, shared food at its very best. Mushrooms really are nature's cups just waiting to be filled. Look for ones that will be two to three small mouthfuls when cooked – wild field mushrooms or the large portobello mushrooms are both ideal. These are very rich, so a crisp fennel salad is the perfect accompaniment.

baked mushrooms with Manchego béchamel

2 teaspoons butter

2 teaspoons plain flour

125 ml full-fat milk

50 g Manchego cheese, finely grated

12 wide, flat field mushrooms

¼ teaspoon smoked Spanish paprika (pimentón)

fennel salad:

1 small fennel bulb

1 handful of fresh flat leaf parsley leaves

2 teaspoons olive oil

2 teaspoons freshly squeezed lemon juice

sea salt and freshly ground black pepper

Serves 4–6

Put the butter in a small saucepan and cook over high heat until it is melted and sizzling. Before the butter burns, add the flour and stir quickly to form a thick paste. Remove from the heat and add a little of the milk, stirring constantly until thick and smooth. Return the pan to medium heat and add the remaining milk, whisking constantly until all the milk is incorporated and the mixture is smooth and thick. Remove from the heat and let cool.

Preheat the oven to 220°C (425°F) Gas 7. Remove the stalks from the mushrooms and sit the mushrooms in a small baking dish, gill-side up. Spoon the cheese sauce into the caps and sprinkle the paprika over the top. Cook in the preheated oven for 20 minutes, until the mushrooms are soft and the sauce is golden and bubbling.

While the mushrooms are cooking, slice the fennel bulb as finely as possible, chop the fronds and put in a bowl with the parsley, oil and lemon juice. Toss to combine, season to taste and serve with the warm mushrooms.

These fun little Chinese dumplings are called potstickers because of the technique of first pan-frying their bottoms until they are crisp and golden, then pouring over stock (or water), quickly covering and letting them steam in the resulting hot vapour. I have used gow gee wrappers here, which are available from Chinese markets. If you can't find them, you can use wonton wrappers.

vegetable potstickers with orange dipping sauce

300 g red cabbage, finely shredded

1 teaspoon sea salt flakes

2 tablespoons vegetable oil, plus about 65 ml for shallow-frying

1 tablespoon finely grated fresh ginger

4 garlic cloves, finely chopped

1 small carrot, grated

1 tablespoon light soy sauce

18 gow gee wrappers

125 ml vegetable stock

4 spring onions, thinly sliced

1 handful of roughly chopped fresh coriander

freshly ground black pepper

orange dipping sauce:

65 ml light soy sauce

65 ml rice vinegar

65 ml freshly squeezed orange juice

Makes 18 small dumplings

To make the dipping sauce, put all of the ingredients in a bowl and whisk to combine. Cover and set aside until ready to serve.

Put the cabbage in a bowl and sprinkle over the sea salt. Cover and let sit for 30 minutes, stirring a few times. Put the cabbage in a colander and squeeze out as much liquid as possible. Tip it onto a chopping board and finely chop. Transfer to a bowl and set aside.

Put the 2 tablespoons oil in a large frying pan or wok and set over high heat. Add the ginger and garlic and stir-fry for just a few seconds to soften the ingredients and flavour the oil. Add the cabbage and carrot and stir-fry for 1 minute. Add the soy sauce and season with black pepper. Transfer to a bowl and let cool.

Put 2 teaspoons of the mixture in the centre of a gow gee wrapper. Brush around the edges with a little water and bring the two sides together to form a half-moon shape, snugly enclosing the filling. Press the edges firmly and crimp or pleat around the edges to seal. Gently tap the dumplings on their base so that they get a flattened bottom. Put the dumplings on a baking tray lined with baking paper, cover and refrigerate until you are ready to cook them.

Cook the potstickers in 2 batches. Put half of the oil for shallow-frying in a non-stick frying pan and set over medium heat. Add the first batch of potstickers to the pan and cook for 2–3 minutes until the bottoms sizzle in the oil and turn crisp and golden. Shake the pan while they are cooking so that they don't stick. Carefully add half of the stock, standing well back from the pan, as it will splutter. Quickly cover with a lid and let cook for 2–3 minutes, until the dumpings are steamed and the filling is cooked through. Cook the second batch in the same way. Sprinkle with coriander and spring onions and serve warm with the orange dipping sauce on the side.

courgette and mint fritters with spicy tomato jam

This is a quick, no-fuss tomato jam. Keep your eye on the chillies – they can be eye-wateringly hot and turn your jam into something only a few die-hards would enjoy. It's best to remove all the seeds initially, then take it from there. This rich-coloured jam is also delicious served with the Spelt Toasts on page 18 and a big chunk of mature Cheddar.

2 courgettes, grated
50 g feta cheese, crumbled
10–12 fresh mint leaves, finely shredded
2 egg whites
1 tablespoon cornflour
3 tablespoons olive oil

spicy tomato jam:
4 ripe tomatoes, halved
1 large red chilli, deseeded and thinly sliced
1 tablespoon olive oil
1 garlic clove, crushed
1 teaspoon white sugar

Makes 12 fritters

To make the jam, preheat the oven to 220°C (425°F) Gas 7. Line a baking tray with baking paper. Put the tomatoes in a bowl with the chilli and oil and toss to coat. Arrange them cut-side up on the prepared tray and cook in the preheated oven for 30 minutes, until just starting to collapse and soften. Transfer them to the bowl of a food processor, add the garlic and sugar and process until smooth. Transfer the mixture to a saucepan and cook over high heat until it boils. Continue to boil for about 10 minutes until the mixture has reduced in volume by half. Spoon into a bowl and let cool.

Put the courgettes, feta and mint in a bowl and stir to combine. In a separate, grease-free bowl, whisk the egg whites until they are white and frothy. Add the cornflour and whisk until the cornflour has dissolved. Tip the courgette mixture into the egg whites and gently fold in until combined.

Heat the oil in a non-stick frying pan over high heat. Cook the fritters in 2 batches. Spoon 1 heaped tablespoon of the mixture into the pan and press down lightly to form a flat fritter. Repeat to create 5 more fritters. Fry for 2 minutes on each side until a dark, golden brown. Carefully lift the cooked fritters onto kitchen paper to drain any excess oil. Repeat this process to make a second batch of 6 fritters. Serve hot with the spicy tomato jam.

tempura of mixed veggies with citrus dipping sauce

Like origami, tempura is often perceived as an art form not to be attempted without a manual. This couldn't be further from the truth. Just follow a few simple rules. Use crisp vegetables without too high a water content (I tried this with endive and lettuce with disappointing results). Iced water is essential, as it ensures the batter is light and lacy. Don't overbeat the batter – a few quick stirs with a chopstick is all that is required and any lumps will just add texture to the cooked batter.

8 asparagus spears, ends trimmed
1 yellow pepper, cut into ½-cm strips
1 red pepper, cut into ½-cm strips
500 ml vegetable oil
50 g cornflour
125 g plain flour
¼ teaspoon baking powder
½ teaspoon salt
325 ml iced water

citrus dipping sauce:
65 ml Japanese soy sauce
1 tablespoon freshly squeezed lemon juice
1 tablespoon freshly squeezed lime juice
1 tablespoon freshly squeezed orange juice

Serves 4

To make the citrus dipping sauce, put all of the ingredients in a small bowl and whisk to combine. Set aside until ready to serve.

Put the prepared vegetables on a plate near to your hob top. Put the oil in a frying pan and set over medium/high heat. Combine the cornflour, plain flour, baking powder and salt in a bowl. Put the iced water in another chilled bowl. Working quickly, add the flour mixture to the cold water, stirring for just a few seconds with a chopstick or a knife, leaving the mixture lumpy-looking.

Cook the tempura in batches. Add a small handful of vegetables to the batter, letting any excess batter drip back into the bowl. Cook for 2–3 minutes, turning often with tongs so that the batter cooks evenly all over and is lightly golden and lacy looking. Put the tempura on some kitchen paper for a minute to absorb any excess oil. Reheat the oil and repeat with the remaining vegetables and batter. Serve warm with the citrus dipping sauce on the side.

See photograph on page 30.

cauliflower and caper berries on halloumi

Cauliflower is transformed when cooked in a generous amount of olive oil with classic Middle Eastern flavourings such as cumin, tahini and lemon juice. I look for any excuse to include delicious halloumi cheese in a recipe, but the cauliflower mixture here could also be served as a topping on crisply toasted sourdough bread. If you enjoy spicy foods, try a light sprinkle of dried chilli flakes for a piquant appetizer. If you are a fan of cauliflower, you could also try the warm Cauliflower and Swiss Chard Salad on page 53.

3 tablespoons olive oil

300 g cauliflower, broken into small florets

2 garlic cloves, chopped

50 g caper berries, large ones halved

100 g green olives, stoned and sliced

3 tablespoons chopped fresh flat leaf parsley

1 tablespoon freshly squeezed lemon juice

2 teaspoons light olive oil

300 g halloumi cheese, cut into ½-cm thick slices

sea salt and freshly ground black pepper

Serves 4–6

Heat the olive oil in a frying pan and cook the cauliflower florets for 8–10 minutes over high heat, stirring often until they brown evenly and start to crisp up. Add the garlic, caper berries, olives, parsley and lemon juice and cook for 2 minutes, stirring constantly. Season to taste and leave in the pan to keep warm.

Heat the light olive oil in a non-stick frying pan set over high heat. Cook the halloumi slices for 1 minute on each side, until golden brown. Transfer the halloumi to serving plates and spoon the warm cauliflower mixture over each one. Serve immediately.

See photograph on page 31.

spicy tomato, black bean and feta dip with organic corn chips

The fresh flavours in this Tex-Mex-style dip seem to have a natural affinity with corn chips. This is a twist on the popular chilli con queso (chilli with cheese), usually made with Cheddar or mozzarella. I find the flavour of Cheddar too overpowering and the texture a little greasy with the mildly spiced flavours here, so I opt for feta instead. It doesn't entirely melt, but softens and adds a salty bite to the dip, which enhances the sweetness of the tomatoes and pepper. If you are in a hurry, you can easily substitute the dried beans with tinned red kidney beans.

90 g dried black beans

1 tablespoon olive oil

1 small red pepper, thinly sliced

1 red onion, thinly sliced

1 teaspoon ground cumin

2 garlic cloves, finely chopped

2 small red chillies, finely chopped

3 tomatoes, chopped

1 tablespoon red wine vinegar

250 ml passata

200 g feta cheese, crumbled

organic corn chips, to serve

Serves 4

Soak the black beans in cold water overnight. Drain and rinse well. Put them in a large saucepan with plenty of water and bring to the boil. Cook for 25–30 minutes, until soft to the bite. Drain well and set aside.

Heat the oil in a saucepan set over high heat and add the red pepper and onion. Reduce the heat to low, cover and cook for about 8 minutes. Add the cumin, garlic and chillies and cook for a further 2 minutes. Add the beans, tomatoes, vinegar and passata and bring to the boil. Reduce the heat and simmer rapidly for about 10 minutes, until almost all the liquid has evaporated and the tomatoes start to look mushy. Transfer to a flame-proof dish and sprinkle the crumbled feta over the top. Cook under a preheated high grill until the cheese is soft and just starting to brown. Serve hot with corn chips on the side for dipping.

This is simple tapas-style food for sharing at its best. The tortilla may not look that substantial, but thanks to the creamy Taleggio cheese, it packs a super-rich taste punch and is more than enough for four to enjoy as a starter or snack. Keep your eyes peeled for nice little new potatoes when you are out shopping. Sometimes you will only be able to find waxies that are the size of a golf ball, but at other times you'll see deliciously nutty little potatoes (the size of a shelled walnut) like the ones I've used here. The red pepper tapenade is a very versatile recipe to have in your repertoire. It can be tossed through cooked pasta, spooned over grilled vegetables and stirred into soup. Try it with the Summer Sweetcorn Soup on page 66.

Taleggio and potato tortilla with red pepper tapenade

10–12 small, waxy new potatoes, thickly sliced

1 small red onion, roughly chopped

1 tablespoon olive oil

250 ml vegetable stock

1 handful of fresh flat leaf parsley, chopped

100 g Taleggio cheese, chopped or torn into large chunks

2 eggs, lightly beaten

red pepper tapenade:

1 large red pepper

1 garlic clove, chopped

50 g pine nuts, lightly toasted

2 tablespoons olive oil

50 g Parmesan cheese, finely grated

Serves 4

To make the tapenade, preheat the oven to 220°C (425°F) Gas 7. Put a baking tray in the oven for a few minutes to heat. Put the red pepper on the tray and cook it in the preheated oven for about 15 minutes, turning often until the skin is starting to blacken and puff up. Transfer it to a clean plastic bag and let cool. When the pepper is cool enough to handle, peel off the skin, roughly tear or chop the flesh and put it in a food processor. Add the garlic, pine nuts and oil and process until smooth. Spoon into a bowl, add the Parmesan and stir well to combine.

Put the potatoes, onion and oil in a frying pan set over high heat and cook for 1 minute. Add the stock and cook for about 10 minutes, until the stock has evaporated and the vegetables start to sizzle in the pan. Stir through the parsley and put the pieces of cheese among the potatoes. Pour the eggs into the pan and cook for 2–3 minutes until they start to puff up around the edges. Give the pan a couple of firm shakes – this will make it easier to get the cooked tortilla out of the pan. Meanwhile, preheat the grill to high. Put the frying pan under the hot grill and cook the tortilla for 1–2 minutes, until the top is golden but still wobbly in the centre. Use a spatula to smear some of the tapenade onto the base of a serving plate and carefully slide the tortilla onto the plate. Cut into 4 slices and eat direct from the plate with extra tapenade on the side.

summer grazing platter

The pumpkin soda bread was really the inspiration for the other little dishes here. This is a no-fuss, dead-easy bread to make and it also freezes and toasts well. I have enjoyed this with cheese and home-made quince paste in cooler months. But here we have the best of summer's bounty – tasty little plates to graze on during a summer's afternoon. Serve with a generous slice of mature Cheddar.

pumpkin and caraway seed soda bread

300 g pumpkin, peeled, deseeded and cut into chunks
1 tablespoon treacle
150 g self-raising wholemeal flour
125 g fine semolina
1 tablespoon caraway seeds
1 teaspoon salt
125 ml soda water

Makes 1 medium loaf

Preheat the oven to 200°C (400°F) Gas 6. Cook the pumpkin in a saucepan of boiling water for 10 minutes until soft when pierced with a skewer. Drain and return to the warm pan. Add the treacle and mash to a chunky paste. Put the flours in a bowl with the caraway seeds and salt and use a whisk to stir to combine. Form a well in the centre and add the pumpkin while it is still warm. Use a large spoon to stir for 1 minute, then gradually stir through the soda water until you have a chunky mix that is just combined. Do not overmix. Working quickly, lightly flour a work surface, turn the dough out and use your hands to form it into an oval. Put the dough on a baking tray dusted with a little fine semolina and use a sharp knife to make 3–4 shallow diagonal slices across the top of the loaf. Bake in the preheated oven for 30 minutes. Open the door to the oven, leaving the oven on and cook for a further 10 minutes. This will give the bread a nice dry crust. Remove from the oven and let cool on a wire rack.

sweetcorn relish

1 tablespoon olive oil
2 fresh corn-on-the-cobs, freshly shucked
1 small red pepper, thinly sliced
1 small red onion, thinly sliced
1 garlic clove, finely chopped
1 tablespoon brown sugar
125 ml vegetable stock
2 teaspoons hot English mustard
125 ml cider vinegar
1 teaspoon cornflour

Serves 4–6

Heat the oil in a frying pan set over high heat and add the corn kernels, red pepper and onion. Cook for 5 minutes, stirring constantly. Add the garlic and cook, stirring, for 1 minute. Stir in the sugar, add the stock and bring to the boil. Reduce the heat and let simmer for about 10 minutes, until almost all the liquid has evaporated.

Put the mustard, vinegar and cornflour in a small bowl and mix well. Add this mixture to the sweetcorn and cook over high heat for 1 minute, until the liquid thickens and coats the sweetcorn. Remove from the heat and let cool before serving.

pickled aubergine

250 ml white wine vinegar
1 aubergine, chopped
1 large red chilli, sliced
1 garlic clove, sliced
½ teaspoon caraway seeds
3 tablespoons olive oil

Makes 375 ml

Put the vinegar in a small saucepan with 500 ml water and bring to the boil. Add the aubergine, cover with a lid and turn off the heat. Let the aubergine sit in the liquid for about 20 minutes. Drain well and let the aubergine cool completely. Put the aubergine in a bowl with the chilli, garlic, caraway seeds and oil. Cover and refrigerate for 1 day before eating.

slow-roasted tomatoes

8 ripe Italian tomatoes, such as Roma, halved
1 tablespoon olive oil
½ teaspoon sea salt
½ teaspoon white sugar
1 teaspoon ground cumin

Serves 4–6

Preheat the oven to 180°C (350°F) Gas 4. Put the tomatoes in a bowl with the other ingredients and toss to coat in the oil. Put the tomatoes, cut-side up, on a baking tray and roast in the preheated oven for 1 hour, until they have shrivelled and are starting to char around the edges. Serve warm.

midweek
meals

This gorgeous-looking and delicious rice dish is inspired by the salade Niçoise, the popular plate from southern France. This version doesn't include the tuna and anchovies, but you can add these if you like. What it does have is generous handfuls of market-fresh herbs and the key flavours of summer-ripe tomatoes, black olives, green beans and hard-boiled eggs.

Niçoise-style brown rice salad with fresh herbs

4 eggs

200 g baby green beans

350 g short-grain brown rice

60 ml olive oil

1 garlic clove, crushed

2 tablespoons freshly squeezed lemon juice

200 g cherry tomatoes, halved

60 g black olives, pitted and halved

1 small of bunch fresh chives, finely snipped

1 large handful of fresh parsley, chopped

1 large handful of fresh basil leaves

1 large handful of fresh mint leaves

1 small handful of fresh tarragon leaves

sea salt and freshly ground black pepper

Serves 4

Put the eggs in a small saucepan and cover with cold water. Set over high heat and bring to the boil. Cook for 3 minutes, then rinse under cold water. When cool enough to handle, peel and halve them then set aside.

Cook the beans in boiling water for 1 minute. Drain and put in a bowl of cold water. Put the rice in a sieve and rinse well under cold running water. Transfer the rice to a large saucepan and add sufficient just-boiled water. Set the pan over high heat, return the water to the boil and cook the rice for 10–12 minutes until it is tender but retains some 'bite'. Tip the rice into a sieve, rinse under cold running water and drain well. Put the rice and drained beans in a large bowl and add the oil, garlic and lemon juice. Stir until the rice is coated in the oil. Add the tomatoes, olives and herbs, toss to combine and season to taste with salt and pepper. Arrange the egg halves on top to serve.

old-fashioned garden salad with garlic toasts

We all have childhood memories of food. I recall that in summer (and this is well and truly before the days of mass-produced salad dressings), a bowl of salad cream would sit on the table ready to be spooned over a simple salad. To my young taste buds, the flavours were at first challenging and then addictive; tangy, creamy and sweet all at once.
I really wanted to capture the spirit of this dressing and my research led me to the recipes of Constance Spry, famous for coronation chicken and, as I discovered, salad cream. I have tweaked the ingredients, making them more modern, but the fresh, summer garden produce is the same and the crisp garlic toasts add a contemporary crunch.

6 thin slices of Italian bread, such as ciabatta
3–4 garlic cloves
1 baby cos lettuce
1 small round butterhead lettuce
1 handful of curly endive or frisée
3 ripe tomatoes
1 bunch of spring onions
200 g mature Cheddar, thinly sliced
2 hard-boiled eggs, quartered
olive oil, for brushing or drizzling

salad cream:
1 teaspoon sea salt flakes
1 teaspoon caster sugar
1 tablespoon mild mustard, such as Dijon
1 tablespoon white wine vinegar
60 ml olive oil
100 ml full-fat milk

Serves 4

To make the salad cream, put the salt, sugar, mustard, vinegar and oil in a bowl and whisk to dissolve the salt and sugar. Begin to add the milk, very slowly at first and whisking the whole time. Continue to add all of the milk until you have a dressing the consistency of a thin custard.

Brush or drizzle a little oil over each side of the bread slices. Lightly toast the bread until golden on both sides and rub the garlic cloves over the toast. Allow the toast to cool and crisp up.

Combine the salad ingredients in a large bowl. Roughly break up the pieces of toast and add to the salad with some of the salad cream then gently toss to combine. Serve immediately.

salad of winter fruit with blue cheese and spinach

I am so happy we have finally moved on from the need to have the perfect red or green apple displayed in the supermarket – row upon row of them, all polished to a high shine and flawless. That said, the vast number of organically grown apple and pear varieties at your local farmers' market might be a little overwhelming! If you are unsure, my tip is to ask your market supplier a few simple questions such as what varieties are good for cooking, for munching on or, as here, slicing directly into a salad bowl with a few other great ingredients. I have chosen firm, woody-looking fruit for this recipe, just how it ought to look when you pick it straight from the tree.

2 apples, cored and cut into thin wedges
2 firm pears, cored and cut into thin wedges
1 small head of radicchio, leaves separated
100 g fresh spinach leaves
200 g firm blue cheese, crumbled

tarragon vinaigrette:
3 tablespoons light olive oil
1 tablespoon tarragon vinegar
¼ teaspoon freshly cracked white pepper
sea salt

Serves 4

Combine the apples, pears, radicchio, spinach and blue cheese in a large salad bowl and toss gently to combine. Whisk the oil, vinegar and pepper in a small bowl and season with a little sea salt. Pour the dressing over the salad, toss well and serve immediately.

See photograph on page 45.

garlic and chilli rice soup with spring greens

This is a substantial soup – really more of a light stew. Boiled rice soups are popular in many Asian countries, especially China where they are called congees. They are often eaten for breakfast, but are an acquired taste as the rice is boiled until it breaks down to form a rather viscous white 'porridge'. Spring greens can be the fresh, young outer leaves of brassicas such as cabbage. They work very nicely with the simple Asian flavours here.

1 tablespoon vegetable oil
2 teaspoons sesame oil
2 garlic cloves, chopped
4 spring onions, finely chopped
2 teaspoons finely grated fresh ginger
1 small red chilli, deseeded and thinly sliced
100 g long-grain white rice
1.5 litres vegetable stock
1 tablespoon soy sauce or Thai fish sauce
1 bunch of spring greens, roughly shredded
1 small bunch of fresh coriander, chopped
white pepper

Serves 2

Put the oils in a saucepan and set over high heat. Add the garlic and spring onions and cook until the garlic is turning golden and just starting to burn. This will give the soup a lovely, nutty garlic flavour. Add the ginger, chilli and rice to the pan and stir-fry in the garlic-infused oil for 1 minute. Add the stock and soy sauce and bring to the boil.

Cover with a lid and cook over low heat for 30 minutes, until the rice is soft and the soup has thickened. Add the spring greens and cook for 5 minutes, until they turn emerald green and are tender. Ladle the soup into warmed serving bowls, sprinkle the coriander over the top and season to taste with pepper.

oven-baked courgette and tomato risotto

This is a super-speedy dish. As with any recipe for a baked risotto, you are not going to get the creamy texture of one cooked by the more conventional method. That said, this recipe more than makes up for it in other ways – take simple, fresh ingredients, a few quick stirs and dinner is ready to serve.

750 ml vegetable stock
2 tablespoons olive oil
1 onion, chopped
1 garlic clove, chopped
330 g short-grain white rice
2 tablespoons fresh rosemary needles
2 courgettes, roughly chopped
2 tomatoes, chopped
50 g butter
50 g Parmesan cheese, finely grated

Serves 4

Preheat the oven to 200°C (400°C) Gas 6. Put the stock in a large saucepan and set over low heat. Put the oil in a flameproof, lidded casserole dish and set over low heat. Add the onion and garlic and fry gently for 2–3 minutes until the onion has softened. Add the rice and the rosemary and cook for a further minute before adding the courgettes. Stir for 1 minute, or until the rice becomes opaque, then add the tomatoes. Pour the hot stock into the casserole and stir well to remove any stuck-on bits and to combine all the ingredients. As soon as the liquid starts to simmer, cover with the lid and cook in the preheated oven for 30 minutes.

Stir through the butter and half of the Parmesan, then sprinkle the remaining Parmesan on top to serve.

See photograph on page 48.

linguine with heirloom tomatoes, red endive and black olives

This pasta recipe involves the Italian technique of gently blanching the garlic in warm oil so that it softens and imparts its flavour without dominating the other fresh ingredients. When it comes to tomatoes, we are spoilt for choice during the summer months, so I like to use a number of interesting varieties, heirloom if possible, and mix up the colours. The bitter red endive leaves offset the fruity sweetness of the tomatoes.

65 ml olive oil
4 garlic cloves, chopped
6 medium tomatoes, roughly chopped
1 red Belgian endive (chicory), leaves torn
1 handful of small black olives
400 g linguine
50 g Parmesan cheese, finely grated
sea salt and freshly ground black pepper

Serves 4

Heat the oil in a large frying pan, add the garlic and cook over medium heat for a couple of minutes, to soften, but don't let it burn. Add the tomatoes to the pan and cook for 2–3 minutes so that they are just soft and starting to break up. Remove from the heat, stir through the endive leaves and olives and season with salt and pepper. Set aside while cooking the pasta.

Cook the pasta according to the packet instructions. Drain well and put in a large bowl. Add the tomato sauce and half of the Parmesan and toss to combine. Serve with extra Parmesan on top.

See photograph on page 49.

braised fennel with polenta

Always buy fennel with the feathery leaves intact, as these can be added to the final stages of a dish or used as a garnish. While smaller, tender bulbs can be eaten raw, the larger, tougher ones are perfect when braised, as here.

2 large fennel bulbs
65 ml light olive oil
1 onion, chopped
2 garlic cloves, chopped
1 small red chilli, chopped
1 handful of fresh flat leaf parsley leaves, roughly chopped
2 tablespoons freshly squeezed lemon juice
2 tablespoons sweet white wine
500 ml vegetable stock
1 handful of small black olives
grated Pecorino cheese, to serve

creamy polenta:
500 ml full-fat milk
1 litre vegetable stock
200 g instant polenta
50 g butter
100 g Pecorino cheese, finely grated

Serves 4

Cut about ½ cm from the gnarly stem on the bottom of the fennel bulbs. Cut off the fronds, chop finely and reserve. Cut off and discard all but about 1 cm from the dark green stems. Thinly slice the remaining white fennel bulb lengthways. Put the oil in a heavy-based saucepan and set over high heat. Add the onions, garlic and chillies and cook for 2–3 minutes until softened. Add the parsley and fennel bulb and fronds and cook for 2–3 minutes, stirring often so that the fennel becomes coated in the oil. Add the lemon juice, wine and stock and bring to the boil. Cover with a lid and turn the heat down to a low simmer for 20 minutes, stirring occasionally. Add the olives, remove the lid and boil rapidly until there is only a little liquid left and the fennel is very soft.

Meanwhile, to make the polenta, put the milk and stock in a saucepan and bring to a gentle simmer over medium heat. Slowly pour in the polenta in a steady stream and beat with a balloon whisk until smooth. Reduce the heat to low and continue to beat for 4–5 minutes. When the mixture thickens, discard the whisk and use a wooden spoon. Add the butter and cheese and stir until melted into the polenta. Spoon some polenta onto serving plates, top with the braised fennel and sprinkle with grated Pecorino to serve.

spaghetti with broccoli, walnuts and ricotta

The light texture and creamy flavour of ricotta cheese makes the perfect backdrop to walnuts and broccoli in this deliciously simple and quick pasta dish.

100 g walnut halves

1 head of broccoli, about 400–500 g

3 tablespoons light olive oil

3 garlic cloves, thinly sliced

1 handful of fresh flat leaf parsley, chopped

finely grated zest and freshly squeezed juice of 1 unwaxed lemon

200 g fresh ricotta cheese

400 g spaghetti

sea salt and freshly ground black pepper

Serves 4

Preheat the oven to 180°C (350°F) Gas 4. Spread the walnuts out on a baking tray and roast in the preheated oven for about 8 minutes, shaking the tray occasionally, until they start to brown.

To prepare the broccoli, trim off the gnarly part, about 2 cm from the stem end, and discard. Thinly slice the stem until you reach the point where it starts to branch into florets. Slice off the individual florets. Heat the oil in a frying pan, add the stems and cook for about 2–3 minutes, turning often, then add the florets and cook for about 5 minutes, until the broccoli has softened. Add the garlic, parsley, lemon zest and walnuts and cook for 5 minutes, stirring often. Reduce the heat to medium and stir through the ricotta and lemon juice. Season well with salt and pepper and leave in the pan to keep warm.

Cook the spaghetti according to the packet instructions. Drain and return it to the warm pan with the sauce. Stir gently to combine and serve immediately.

cauliflower and Swiss chard salad

The distinctive thick leaves that seem to hug the head of a cauliflower are actually protecting the white 'flower' from the sun. In doing so, they deprive it of what it needs to turn green, and that's essentially the difference between the cauliflower and its close relative broccoli. I'm a huge fan of the cauliflower, but it is so often overlooked in favour of other brassicas, such as broccoli, that are quicker to cook. I like its intense flavour and use it often in creamy soups and curries or, as I have done here, in a light and spicy Middle Eastern-style salad.

65 ml light olive oil

1 small head of cauliflower, separated into large florets

1 teaspoon ground cumin

6 large Swiss chard leaves, chopped into 2-cm wide strips

1 red onion, cut into wedges

2 garlic cloves, chopped

400-g tin chickpeas, rinsed and drained

65 ml tahini (sesame seed paste)

2 tablespoons freshly squeezed lemon juice

¼ teaspoon freshly cracked white pepper

sea salt

Serves 4

Put the oil in a frying pan set over high heat, add the cauliflower florets and cook for 8–10 minutes, turning often, until they are a dark, golden brown. Add the cumin and cook, stirring, for 1 minute. Add the Swiss chard, onion and garlic to the pan and cook for a further 2–3 minutes. Add the chickpeas and stir. Season to taste with salt.

Combine the tahini, lemon juice and white pepper in a small bowl and add a little salt to taste. Whisk to combine. Transfer the vegetables to a bowl and drizzle the dressing over the top to serve.

See photograph on page 54.

tenderstem broccoli, shiitake and tofu omelette

This is an omelette with a distinctly Asian feel with creamy cubes of tofu replacing the more traditional cheese. This is perfect for a light, midweek supper, but I've occasionally enjoyed it as a weekend brunch. As a variation, you can replace the broccoli with young, tender peas and add a sprinkling of fresh coriander.

1 tablespoon light olive oil

2 shallots, sliced

1 bunch of tenderstem broccoli, chopped into small pieces

200 g shiitake mushrooms

50 g baby spinach leaves

2 teaspoons light soy sauce

300 g firm tofu, cubed

8 eggs, lightly beaten

ground white pepper

oyster sauce, to serve (optional)

Serves 4

Put the oil in a large, non-stick frying pan and set over high heat. Add the shallots, broccoli and mushrooms and stir-fry for 3–4 minutes, until the mushrooms are soft and the broccoli turns a bright, emerald green. Add the spinach and cook until just wilted. Add the soy sauce and stir. Arrange the cubes of tofu over the vegetables so that they are evenly spaced. Preheat the grill to high. Pour the beaten eggs into the pan and cook over high heat until the edges have puffed up.

Keep the omelette in the pan, place it under the preheated grill and cook until golden and firm on top. Remove and let cool a little before drizzling with the oyster sauce (if using), then sprinkle with white pepper to serve.

See photograph on page 55.

asparagus, sweetcorn and goats' cheese frittata

The frittata is a brilliant stand-by for a no-fuss, fast supper. It's an Italian-style omelette, often cooked slowly and still slightly moist when served, but I like to eat mine a little firmer, so flash it under a hot grill. Crunchy asparagus and sweetcorn work nicely here combined with farm-fresh eggs, creamy goats' cheese and fresh, tangy dill.

2 bunches of thin asparagus spears

2 fresh corn-on-the-cobs

50 g butter

4 spring onions, finely chopped

1 handful of fresh dill, chopped

8 eggs, beaten

200 g firm goats' cheese, broken into pieces

sea salt and freshly ground black pepper

Serves 4

Trim, or snap off, the woody ends from the asparagus and cut the spears into 2–3-cm pieces. Shuck the corn kernels from the cobs.

Heat half of the butter in a large non-stick frying pan set over medium heat. Add the asparagus, sweetcorn and spring onions and fry for 2–3 minutes, stirring often. Transfer the vegetables to a large bowl and add the dill, reserving a little to use as garnish. Wipe the pan clean. Add the beaten eggs to the vegetables, gently stirring to combine, and season well with salt and pepper.

Preheat the grill to high. Put the remaining butter in the pan and set over high heat. Swirl the pan around as the butter melts so that it coats the bottom and just starts to sizzle. Pour the frittata mixture into the pan and reduce the heat to medium. Arrange the pieces of goats' cheese over the top of the frittata and gently push them into the mixture. Cook for about 8 minutes, until the sides of the frittata start to puff up (reduce the heat if the bottom appears to be cooking too quickly).

Keep the fritatta in the pan and place it under the preheated grill. Cook for 1 minute only just to set the top. Let cool a little in the pan, sprinkle with the reserved dill and serve immediately.

farfalle pasta with asparagus, soft-boiled duck eggs and Parmesan

You can of course use hen's eggs here, but duck eggs are a bit of a treat and can easily be found at farmers' markets. They are slightly larger and have a rich flavour. They also make the best breakfast – simply soft-boiled and served with fingers of hot, buttered toast. Do use fine asparagus for this recipe; fresh and tender young spears that have been grown locally and haven't travelled too far would be best as, once picked, their sweetness fades fast.

4 duck eggs or 6 hen's eggs
2 bunches of thin asparagus spears
2 tablespoons olive oil
2 garlic cloves, chopped
250 ml single cream
400 g farfalle or other pasta of your choice
50 g Parmesan cheese, finely grated
2 handfuls of wild rocket leaves
sea salt and freshly ground black pepper

Serves 4

Put the eggs in a saucepan and pour in sufficient cold water to cover. Bring to the boil over high heat and cook for 5 minutes. Drain and run the eggs under cold water until the shells are cool enough to handle. Set aside.

Trim or snap any woody ends off the asparagus and cut the spears into 2-cm lengths. Put the oil in a frying pan and set over high heat. Add the asparagus and cook for 2 minutes, stirring constantly. Add the garlic and cook for another minute, then add the cream to the pan. Remove from the heat and let sit so that the garlic flavours the cream.

Cook the farfalle according to the packet instructions. Drain and return it to the warm pan with the asparagus sauce. Peel and roughly chop the eggs. The yolks will be soft, so quickly add these to the warm pasta with the Parmesan and rocket. Season well with salt and pepper and stir gently to combine. Serve immediately.

mushrooms with bay leaves and lemon on toast

At farmers' markets you will often see a stall that sells just mushrooms. This is because they require unique growing conditions and many growers will dedicate themselves to growing nothing else – these guys really know their mushrooms! I have used meaty field mushrooms here, as they keep their shape when cooked and can hold their own against the quietly intense flavour of bay leaves.

2 tablespoons light olive oil
2 bay leaves
2 strips of lemon zest
500 g large, flat field mushrooms, thinly sliced
2 garlic cloves, sliced
1 handful of fresh flat leaf parsley, chopped
1 tablespoon freshly squeezed lemon juice
4 slices of sourdough bread, lightly toasted
sea salt and freshly ground black pepper

Serves 4

Put the oil in a frying pan and set it over high heat. Add the mushrooms and cook for 8–10 minutes, turning them often. Add the bay leaves and lemon zest to the pan and cook for 1 minute to just flavour the mushrooms. Add the garlic and parsley, stir and cook for 1 minute, making sure that the garlic does not burn. Add the lemon juice and season well with salt and pepper.

Spoon the mushroom mixture onto the slices of toasted sourdough bread and serve immediately.

spaghetti with butternut squash, sage and pecorino

This tasty pasta is inspired by the classic Italian dish of pumpkin-filled ravioli with sage butter except this is my inside-out version and therefore much easier to make! I've used butternut squash here, but you could use any winter squash, including pumpkin.

65 ml light olive oil

400 g butternut squash, peeled, deseeded and cut into thin wedges

2 garlic cloves, chopped

10–12 small fresh sage leaves

400 g spaghetti

1 handful of fresh flat leaf parsley, chopped

50 g Pecorino cheese, grated

sea salt and freshly ground black pepper

Serves 4

Put the oil in a frying pan and set over high heat. Add the squash and cook for 5–6 minutes, turning often, until golden but not breaking up. Add the garlic and sage to the pan and cook for 2–3 minutes. Remove from the heat and let sit to allow the flavours to develop.

Cook the pasta according to the packet instructions. Drain well and return to the warm pan with the squash mixture. Add the parsley and half of the Pecorino and season well with salt and pepper. Serve immediately with the remaining cheese sprinkled over the top.

soups and stews

roasted vegetable stock

I have often been disappointed with vegetable stock made in the classic way. Roasted vegetables are more flavoursome, so I prefer to use these as a base for stock. It's not necessary to follow this recipe to the letter. You could add almost anything you have to hand to this basic stock – some leftover tomato stalks, the green parts of leeks you usually discard, mushroom stalks, even parsley stalks left over over when you have used just the leaves for a recipe.

3 tablespoons light olive oil
4–6 garlic cloves, unpeeled
2 large, ripe tomatoes, roughly chopped
2 leeks, sliced
2 carrots, chopped
3 celery sticks, chopped
1 fennel bulb, chopped
4 field mushrooms
1 bunch of fresh parsley stalks
1 tablespoon black peppercorns
sea salt (optional)

Makes about 1 litre

Preheat the oven to 180ºC (350ºF) Gas 4. Put the oil and garlic in a roasting tray and heat in the oven for 10 minutes, until the oil is hot. Carefully add the vegetables to the tray and toss until coated in the hot oil. Return the tray to the oven and roast the vegetables for 1 hour, then turn them and cook for a further 15–30 minutes.

Transfer the vegetables and any of the oil from the tray to a large saucepan and add the parsley stalks, peppercorns and 3 litres cold water. Bring to the boil, then reduce the heat and let gently simmer for about 45 minutes. Pass the mixture through a fine sieve and add a little salt if liked.

The stock will keep for up to 5 days in an airtight container stored in the fridge or it can be frozen.

roasted tomato soup with rarebit toasts

The tomato is held in high regard in the Mediterranean countries, where a second-rate tomato is simply not an option! Many dishes that feature them have few other ingredients, so it's essential that the tomatoes themselves taste good. Dishes such as the Italian salad panzanella need not only the flesh but the juice of ripe tomatoes for the dressing, and Spanish salmorejo, a cold tomato and bread soup, is dependent on the tastiest of the summer crop. Buy your tomatoes in summer from a farmers' market and you can be assured of their quality.

1 kg Italian tomatoes, such as Roma, halved
2 small red onions, quartered
6 sprigs of fresh lemon thyme
1 teaspoon white sugar
1 teaspoon sea salt
2 garlic cloves, sliced
2 tablespoons olive oil
500 ml vegetable stock
sea salt and freshly ground black pepper

rarebit toast fingers:
100 g mature Cheddar cheese
3 tablespoons wheat beer
1 tablespoon Worcestershire sauce
4 slices of wholemeal bread or baguette

Serves 4

Preheat the oven to 170ºC (325ºF) Gas 3. Put the tomatoes, onion, lemon thyme, sugar, salt, garlic and oil in a large bowl. Use your hands to toss the ingredients to combine and evenly coat them in the oil. Tip the mixture out onto a baking tray and roast in the preheated oven for 1½ hours. Discard the lemon thyme sprigs then put the tomatoes, onions and any tasty juices in a food processor or blender and process until smooth, adding a little stock if the mixture is too thick to process. Transfer to a large saucepan, add the stock and cook over gentle heat for 10 minutes. Season to taste and keep warm.

Preheat the grill to high. Put the Cheddar, beer and Worcestershire sauce in a small saucepan set over low heat. Stir until the cheese has melted and the mixture is smooth. Toast the bread under the preheated grill on one side only. Spread about 2 tablespoons of the cheese mixture on each untoasted side of bread and grill until it is bubbling and golden. Cut into fingers and serve with the soup.

Buying locally grown or sourced foods is today's message but it has actually been over 30 years since chef Alice Waters pioneered this philosophy by using her Californian restaurant to promote organic and small farm products, and in doing so helped to establish growers' markets. This ethos resonates here in this simple recipe – to really savour its delightful sweetness, sweetcorn should be eaten really fresh, so do try and get your hands on cobs still wrapped in their husks and no more than a day or two from the field.

summer sweetcorn soup

8 fresh corn-on-the-cobs

1 onion, chopped

1 celery stick, chopped

2 garlic cloves, chopped

40 g butter

1.5 litres vegetable stock

125 ml single cream

Red Pepper Tapenade (see page 35), to serve (optional)

1 small bunch of fresh chives, snipped

sea salt and freshly ground black pepper

crusty bread, to serve

Serves 4

Carefully shuck the corn kernels from the cobs and put them in a large saucepan. Add the onion, celery, garlic and butter and season well with salt and pepper. Set over medium heat and partially cover with a lid. Cook for 10 minutes, shaking the pan often. Add the stock, bring to the boil and let boil for 15 minutes. Remove from the heat and let cool for about 20 minutes.

Transfer the mixture to a food processor or blender and whizz until smooth. You may need to do this in batches. Force the mixture through a fine sieve and return it to a clean saucepan. Add the cream and gently reheat, stirring constantly.

Ladle the soup into warmed serving bowls, top with a dollop of Red Pepper Tapenade (if using), sprinkle with chives and serve with thick slices of good, crusty bread.

slow-cooked onion and cider soup with Gruyère toasts

I couldn't begin to imagine cooking without onions – they are so versatile. The soft and sweet onion mixture here could be added to an egg custard and baked in a pastry case with some soft goats' cheese to make a savoury tart, or spread on a pizza base and topped with black olives and fresh thyme for a classic French pissaladière.

50 g butter

1 kg onions, sliced

4 garlic cloves

1 litre vegetable stock

375 ml sweet cider

2 egg yolks

4 thin slices of baguette or similar

100 g Gruyère cheese, thinly sliced

Serves 4

Put the butter in a saucepan set over medium heat. Add the onions and garlic, partially cover with a lid and cook for 20 minutes, stirring often so that the onions become silky soft without burning. Add the stock and cider and bring to the boil. Reduce heat to low and cook for 40 minutes, until the soup is thick and golden. Remove from the heat and slowly whisk in the egg yolks. Cover and keep warm.

Preheat the grill to high. Toast the bread under the hot grill until lightly golden on one side only. Put the Gruyère slices on the untoasted side and cook under the grill until the cheese is golden brown and bubbling. Ladle the soup into warmed serving bowls and sit a Gruyère toast on top of each to serve.

barley risotto with spring greens and radicchio

You will often see spring greens and radicchio displayed side by side at farmers' markets – both look appealing, especially the boldly coloured radicchio, the 'painted lady' of the lettuce world. When used raw in salads it can be a little too bitter for my liking, but when cooked in this risotto its flavour is softened and the barley adds a nutty note.

220 g pearl barley

2 tablespoons light olive oil

500 g spring greens, roughly chopped

4 large radicchio leaves, torn

finely grated zest and freshly squeezed juice of 1 unwaxed lemon

1.25 litres vegetable stock

25 g butter

1 leek, thinly sliced

2 garlic cloves, chopped

2 teaspoons fresh thyme leaves

1 tablespoon fresh rosemary needles

50 g Parmesan cheese, finely grated, plus extra to serve

1 handful of fresh flat leaf parsley, chopped

Serves 4

Put the barley in a large, heatproof bowl and add sufficient boiling water to cover. Let sit for 10 minutes, just to soften the barley a little, then drain well and set aside.

Put the oil in a frying pan set over medium heat. Add the spring greens and radicchio and cook for 10 minutes, stirring often, until the leaves soften. Add the lemon zest and juice, stir well and set aside. Put the stock in a large saucepan set over low heat and gently warm through while you start the risotto.

Put half of the butter in a saucepan set over medium heat. Add the leek and garlic and cook for 4–5 minutes until the leeks are soft and silky. Add the barley and herbs and stir for 1 minute. Add a ladleful of the warmed stock and cook, stirring constantly, until almost all the stock has been absorbed. Repeat the process until all the stock has been incorporated and the barley is almost cooked through – the risotto will be quite wet. Add the spring greens, radicchio, remaining butter and Parmesan to the pan and stir well to combine. Sprinkle with the parsley and serve with extra Parmesan on the side for sprinkling.

See photograph on page 70.

miso with ramen noodles and stir-fried vegetables

Japanese broths are hearty and comforting. They are often full of fresh and earthy cold-weather vegetables, sometimes with the addition of freshly shucked sweetcorn. The broths themselves are generally made with a base of simple stock and soy sauce or miso. This prepared, soya bean paste is probably the most essential Japanese food item with a very strong 'unami' (savoury) flavour component. Easily found in the Asian foods aisle at your supermarket or a speciality food store, it will keep for ages in your refrigerator. The noodles, although common in Japan, are Chinese wheat-based noodles and, when bought dried, are a very handy staple.

3 tablespoons red miso paste

1 tablespoon light soy sauce

½ teaspoon white sugar

1.25 litres vegetable stock

200 g ramen or thin egg noodles

1 tablespoon light olive oil

2 teaspoons sesame oil

2 teaspoons finely sliced fresh ginger

2 shallots, thinly sliced

2 leeks, julienned

200 g Savoy cabbage leaves, finely shredded

200 g red cabbage, finely shredded

Serves 4

Combine the miso, soy sauce, sugar and stock in a large saucepan set over medium heat and warm until the miso has completely dissolved. Keep warm over low heat. Cook the noodles according to the packet instructions. Drain well and divide between 4 warmed serving bowls.

Put the oils in a wok or large frying pan set over high heat. Add the ginger and shallots and cook for just a few seconds to flavour the oil. Add the leeks and cabbage and stir-fry for 2 minutes, until the vegetables are crisp and glistening with oil.

Ladle the warm miso mixture over the noodles and top with the stir-fried vegetables. Serve immediately.

See photograph on page 71.

smoky hotpot of great northern beans

This is a hearty hotpot packed with autumnal vegetables and rich with smoky paprika. Great northern beans are large and white, resembling butter beans in shape but with a distinctive, delicate flavour. They are widely grown in Midwest America, where they are used in baked dishes. If you can't find them, large butter beans will do just as well.

100 g dried great northern or butter beans

2 tablespoons olive oil

1 large onion, chopped

2 garlic cloves, chopped

2 teaspoons smoked Spanish paprika (pimentón)

1 celery stick, chopped

1 carrot, chopped

2 medium waxy potatoes, cut into 2-cm dice

1 red pepper, chopped

500 ml vegetable stock

sea salt and freshly ground black pepper

crusty bread, to serve

Serves 4

Soak the dried beans in cold water for at least 6 hours or ideally overnight. Drain and put in a large saucepan with sufficient just-boiled water to cover. Cook for 30 minutes until softened. Drain and set aside until needed.

Put the oil in a saucepan set over medium heat. Add the onion and cook for 4–5 minutes until softened. Add the garlic and paprika to the pan and stir-fry for 2 minutes. Add the celery, carrot, potatoes and red pepper and cook for 2 minutes, stirring constantly to coat the vegetables in the flavoured oil. Add the stock and beans and bring to the boil. Reduce the heat and partially cover the pan with a lid. Let simmer for 40 minutes, stirring often, until all the vegetables are cooked. Season to taste and serve with crusty bread for dipping in the sauce.

This technique of cooking rice is a particular favourite of mine. Although Middle Eastern in origin, it has spread far and wide – similar rice dishes can be found in European, Asian, Latin American, Caribbean and Indian cuisines, and it is known by many names including pilaf, pilav and pulao.

orange vegetable and spring onion pilau

2 tablespoons light olive oil

1 onion, chopped

2 garlic cloves, chopped

1 tablespoon finely grated fresh ginger

1 large red chilli, finely chopped

1 teaspoon ground coriander

1 teaspoon ground cumin

1 teaspoon turmeric

50 g flaked almonds

300 g basmati rice

1 carrot, cut into large chunks

200 g pumpkin or squash, peeled, deseeded and cut into wedges

1 small sweet potato, peeled and cut into thick half-circles

freshly squeezed juice of 1 lime

1 handful of fresh coriander leaves, chopped

Serves 4

Put the oil in a heavy-based saucepan set over high heat. Add the onion, garlic, ginger and chilli and cook for 5 minutes, stirring often. Add the spices and almonds and cook for a further 5 minutes, until the spices become aromatic and look very dark in the pan.

Add the rice and cook for a minute, stirring well to coat the rice in the spices. Add the carrot, pumpkin and sweet potato to the pan. Pour in 600 ml water and stir well, loosening any grains of rice that are stuck to the bottom of the pan. Bring to the boil, then reduce the heat to low, cover with a tight-fitting lid and cook for 25 minutes, stirring occasionally.

Add the lime juice and coriander, stir well to combine and serve.

I like to define minestrone as a hotchpotch of whatever takes your fancy. Often thought of as cold weather fare, this version has summer written all over it and is packed with fresh tomatoes and green beans as well as chickpeas, a staple my pantry would never be without. As if it weren't already summery enough, I have added a few handfuls of rocket. Its peppery bite and fresh taste lightens the soup, while making it much more than just another minestrone.

chickpea, tomato and green bean minestrone

2 tablespoons olive oil

1 onion, chopped

2 garlic cloves, chopped

400-g tin chickpeas, rinsed and drained

100 g green beans, sliced on the angle

6 ripe tomatoes, halved

1 handful of chopped fresh flat leaf parsley

1.5 litres vegetable stock

100 g wholemeal spaghetti, broken into 3–4-cm pieces

50 g wild rocket leaves

50 g Pecorino or Parmesan cheese, finely grated

sea salt and freshly ground black pepper

crusty bread, to serve

Serves 4

Put the oil in a large saucepan set over medium heat. Add the onion, partially cover with a lid and cook for 4–5 minutes, stirring often, until softened. Add the garlic and cook for 1 minute. Add the chickpeas, green beans, tomatoes, parsley, stock and spaghetti and bring to the boil.

Reduce the heat and let simmer for 40 minutes, stirring often, until the pasta is cooked and the soup is thick. Season to taste with salt and pepper.

Just before serving, add the rocket and gently stir until the rocket softens. Ladle into warmed serving bowls and sprinkle a generous amount of grated Pecorino over the top. Serve immediately with chunks of crusty bread.

Next time: Try making this delicious soup with different vegetables. Courgettes and carrots are a nice addition but remember that both take a little longer to cook so dice them very finely before adding to the soup with the other vegetables. A pinch of smoky Spanish paprika (pimentón) will add a slightly different flavour.

sweet potato and coconut soup with Thai pesto

Sweet potatoes make an excellent ingredient for soups. When blended they take on a velvety, creamy texture. Here, their sweetness is cut through with some full-on and spicy Asian flavours in the form of a Thai-style pesto, which really brings this soup to life.

1 tablespoon light olive oil

500 g sweet potato, peeled and chopped into chunks

1 red onion, chopped

1 tablespoon Thai red curry paste

500 ml vegetable stock

500 ml coconut milk

Thai pesto:

100 g unsalted peanuts, lightly toasted

2 garlic cloves, chopped

2 teaspoons finely grated fresh ginger

2 large green chillies, deseeded and chopped

1 small bunch of fresh coriander

1 large handful of fresh mint leaves

1 large handful of fresh basil leaves

2 tablespoons light soy sauce or Thai fish sauce

2 tablespoons freshly squeezed lime juice

1 tablespoon soft light brown sugar

Serves 4

Put the oil in a heavy-based saucepan set over medium heat. Add the sweet potato and onion, partially cover with a lid and cook for 15 minutes, stirring often, until they are soft and just starting to turn golden. Increase the heat to high, add the curry paste and stir-fry with the sweet potato for 3–4 minutes so that the paste cooks and becomes fragrant. Add the stock and coconut milk and bring to the boil. Transfer the mixture to a food processor or blender and whizz until smooth. Return the soup to a clean saucepan.

To make the pesto, put all of the ingredients in a food processor or blender and whizz, occasionally scraping down the sides of the bowl, until you have a chunky green paste and the ingredients are all evenly chopped. Gently reheat the soup, then ladle into warmed serving bowls. Top with a generous spoonful of Thai pesto to serve.

spiced cauliflower with red pepper and peas

I think that the vegetarian recipes you find in Indian cuisine are some of the most delicious in the world. Many of the recipes seem to embrace my philosophy of cooking fresh produce at its best, keeping it simple and letting the flavours speak for themselves – good honest cooking. This is a spicy treat that's perfect if you like things hot.

½ head of cauliflower, cut into large florets

2 teaspoons ground cumin

1 teaspoon turmeric

3 tablespoons light olive oil

2 teaspoons black mustard seeds

6–8 curry leaves

1 onion, sliced

1 small red pepper, thinly sliced

1 tablespoon finely grated fresh ginger

2 garlic cloves, chopped

1 large green chilli, sliced

125 ml vegetable stock

2 ripe tomatoes, chopped

125 g freshly shelled peas

steamed or boiled basmati rice, to serve (optional)

Serves 4

Put the cauliflower florets in a large bowl with the cumin and turmeric and toss until evenly coated in the spices.

Put the oil in a frying pan set over medium/high heat. Add the cauliflower, mustard seeds and curry leaves and cook for 8–10 minutes, turning the pieces often so that they soften and colour with the spices. Add the onion and red pepper and cook for 5 minutes. Add the ginger, garlic and chilli and stir-fry for 1 minute, then add the stock, tomatoes and peas. Reduce the heat and let simmer gently for 10 minutes until the vegetables are tender and cooked through.

Spoon over basmati rice to serve, if liked.

See photograph on page 80.

creamy vegetable and cashew curry

The vibrant colours of Kerala, India's southern-most state, are all here on a plate. This deliciously creamy curry is made even richer with the addition of that irresistably moreish snack, the cashew nut.

2 tablespoons vegetable oil

125 g large, unsalted cashews

6 shallots, peeled and halved

1 teaspoon black mustard seeds

6–8 curry leaves

2 garlic cloves, chopped

1 tablespoon finely grated fresh ginger

1 teaspoon turmeric

4 large dried red chillies

1 small red pepper, thinly sliced

2 ripe tomatoes, quartered

8 very small new potatoes, halved

400-ml can coconut milk

steamed or boiled basmati rice, to serve (optional)

Serves 4

Put the oil in a heavy-based saucepan set over medium heat. Add the cashews and shallots and cook for 5 minutes, stirring often, until the cashew are just starting to brown. Add the mustard seeds and curry leaves and cook until the seeds start to pop. Add the garlic, ginger, turmeric, chillies and red pepper to the pan and stir-fry for 2 minutes, until aromatic.

Add the tomatoes, potatoes and coconut milk, partially cover the pan and let simmer gently over low heat for about 20 minutes, or until the potatoes are cooked through. Spoon over basmati rice to serve, if liked.

See photograph on page 81.

Napolitana lentil stew

I use the term Napolitana here to loosely describe the predominance of tomatoes in this Mediterranean-style stew although the flavours could easily be described as Greek, given the inclusion of fresh oregano and feta. There are few ingredients in this dish, so the tomatoes must be of premium quality and vine-ripened in the summer sun.

100 g green or brown lentils

3 tablespoons olive oil

1 onion, chopped

2 garlic cloves, chopped

a small handful of fresh oregano, chopped

1 teaspoon dried chilli flakes

1½ tablespoons salted capers, rinsed

2 ripe tomatoes, roughly chopped

250 ml passata

60 g small black olives

100 g feta cheese, crumbled

crusty bread, to serve

Serves 4

Put the lentils in a large saucepan, add sufficient cold water to cover and set over high heat. Bring to the boil, then reduce the heat and let simmer for 20 minutes until the lentils are tender but retain a little 'bite'. Drain and set aside until needed.

Put the oil in a saucepan set over high heat. Add the onion, garlic, oregano and chilli flakes and cook for 5 minutes, stirring often, until the onion softens. Add the capers, tomatoes, passata, lentils and 250 ml water. Bring to the boil, then reduce the heat and let simmer gently for 10 minutes, stirring occasionally.

Spoon into warmed serving dishes, top with the olives and crumbled feta and serve with crusty bread on the side for dipping into the rich sauce.

Aubergine is probably the vegetable I cook with most often, as it works so well with all of my favourite Asian and Mediterranean flavours. So many iconic international meat-free dishes are based on aubergine, such as the spicy Middle Eastern dip baba ghanoush, Sicilian caponata and the French classic ratatouille. I also like colour in food and this recipe does not disappoint on that score.

aubergine, tomato and red lentil curry

3 tablespoons light olive oil

1 large aubergine, cut into 8 pieces

1 red onion, chopped

2 garlic cloves, chopped

1 tablespoon finely chopped fresh ginger

250 g cherry tomatoes on the vine

6–8 curry leaves

1 teaspoon ground cumin

¼ teaspoon chilli powder

1 tablespoon tomato purée

125 g red split lentils

1 handful of fresh coriander, roughly chopped

boiled or steamed basmati rice, to serve (optional)

Serves 4

Heat the oil in a frying pan set over high heat. When the oil is smoking hot add the aubergine to the pan and cook for 5 minutes, turning the pieces often so that they cook evenly. At first the aubergine will absorb the oil, but as it cooks to a dark and golden colour, the oil will start to seep out back into the pan. Remove the aubergine from the pan at this point and not before.

Add the remaining oil, onions, garlic and ginger to the pan and cook for 5 minutes. Add the cherry tomatoes and cook for 1 minute, until they just soften and collapse, then remove them from the pan before they break up too much and set aside with the aubergine.

Add the curry leaves and cumin to the pan and cook for a couple of minutes as the curry leaves pop and crackle. Add the chilli powder, tomato purée, 480 ml water and the lentils and simmer for 15–20 minutes, until the lentils are tender but retain some 'bite'. Stir in the aubergine and cherry tomatoes and cook the curry for a couple of minutes just to warm through. Stir in the coriander and spoon over basmati rice to serve, if liked.

saturday night
suppers

antipasto sharing plate

These delicious Italian-style antipasti are the perfect solution to entertaining friends. The Italians have a special way with vegetables – no wonder, when their produce is so ripe and full of flavour. Serve this sharing plate with a selection of tasty Italian breads and some fruity olive oil for dipping.

marinated mushrooms

500 ml dry white wine
250 ml white wine vinegar
2 bay leaves
1 teaspoon white sugar
500 g button mushrooms
2 tablespoons olive oil
1 garlic clove, crushed
1 teaspoon finely grated lemon zest from an unwaxed lemon
2 tablespoons freshly squeezed lemon juice
½ teaspoon dried chilli flakes
1 handful of fresh flat leaf parsley leaves, chopped
sea salt

Serves 6–8 sharing

Put the wine and vinegar in a large saucepan set over high heat and add the bay leaves, sugar and 1 teaspoon salt. Bring to the boil, add the mushrooms and let them poach in the hot liquid for 4–5 minutes. Remove with a slotted spoon and drain on kitchen paper. Put the mushrooms in a bowl.

Combine the oil, garlic, lemon zest and juice, chilli flakes and parsley in a bowl and pour over the mushrooms while they are still warm. Cover and let sit for at least 3 hours to allow the flavours to develop, stirring often. Season to taste with salt before serving.

wilted spinach with fried garlic

1 kg fresh baby spinach leaves
65 ml light olive oil
6 garlic cloves, thinly sliced
sea salt and freshly ground black pepper

Serves 6–8 sharing

Bring a large saucepan of lightly salted water to the boil and add the spinach. Cook for 1 minute, until the leaves wilt and turn emerald green. Drain and rinse with cold running water. Drain well and use your hands to squeeze out as much liquid as possible then transfer to a bowl. Heat the oil in a frying pan set over medium/high heat. When the oil starts to smoke, remove the pan from the heat and add the garlic, stirring constantly, until it turns golden. Pour the oil and fried garlic over the spinach and toss to coat evenly in the oil. Season well with salt and pepper. Let sit for about 20 minutes to allow the flavours to develop before serving.

smoky aubergine dip

1 large aubergine
125 ml Greek yoghurt
1 teaspoon ground cumin
1 tablespoon freshly squeezed lemon juice
1 teaspoon sea salt
½ teaspoon ground white pepper
smoked Spanish paprika (pimentón), for sprinkling

Preheat the oven to 220°C (425°F) Gas 7. Prick the aubergine all over with the prongs of a fork. Sit it on the middle shelf of the preheated oven and bake for about 15 minutes, turning once or twice, until the skin is puffed up all over. Let the aubergine sit until it has collapsed and softened.

When cool enough to handle, peel off the skin (leaving a few small charred bits to add a smoky flavour). Put the flesh in a food processor and add the yoghurt, cumin, lemon juice, salt and pepper and process until smooth. Transfer to a serving bowl and sprinkle with paprika to serve.

baked courgette flowers

100 g fresh ricotta cheese
50 g soft feta cheese
1 teaspoon fresh thyme leaves
12 small courgette flowers
2 tablespoons olive oil
2 teaspoons freshly squeezed lemon juice
sea salt and freshly ground black pepper

Makes 12

Preheat the oven to 180°C (350°F) Gas 4 and lightly oil an ovenproof baking dish. Put the ricotta and feta in a bowl and add the thyme. Season well with salt and pepper. Carefully separate the petals of the courgette flowers and pick out the stamens. Put about 1 teaspoon of the cheese mixture into each flower and bring the petals together, gently twisting them to seal the cheese inside. Put the flowers in the baking dish so that they fit snugly and drizzle over the oil and lemon juice. Bake in the preheated oven for about 15–20 minutes until the stems have softened and the cheese is starting to ooze out. Serve immediately or they will spoil.

A Greek salad is a bit like any other iconic salad in that everyone has their own version. In my recipe the feta cheese is kept separate and used only in the creamy dressing. The dressing is also great served with simply grilled or barbecued vegetables or as dip for crunchy, raw vegetables such as peppers, carrots and celery. Lavash is a Lebanese flatbread – if you can't easily find it, use Greek-style pita bread instead.

Greek salad with creamy feta dressing and lavash crisps

200 g lavash or pita bread, torn into pieces

500 g mixed, ripe tomatoes, large ones cut into bite-sized pieces

1 small red pepper, sliced

1 small yellow pepper, sliced

1 cucumber, sliced

1 red onion, thinly sliced

90 g small black olives

2 handfuls of fresh mint leaves

3 tablespoons olive oil

creamy feta dressing:

100 g feta cheese, crumbled

2 garlic cloves, crushed

1 tablespoon white wine vinegar

1 tablespoon finely chopped fresh dill

3 tablepoons light olive oil

125 ml full-fat milk

Serves 4

To make the dressing, put the feta, garlic, vinegar, dill and oil in a food processor or blender and whizz until the mixture is well combined and thick. With the motor still running, add the milk in a steady stream until the mixture is smooth and creamy. Do not overmix. Set the dressing aside until needed.

Preheat the oven to 170°C (325°F) Gas 3. Put the lavash pieces on a baking tray and bake in the preheated oven for 10 minutes. Transfer to a wire rack, arranging them in a single layer, and let cool.

Put the tomatoes, peppers, cucumber, onion, olives, mint and oil in a large bowl and gently toss to combine. Just before serving, add the lavash crisps, toss again and serve with the feta dressing on the side for drizzling.

chilli roasted vegetables with soft goats' cheese

This is a stunning summer dish and I get hungry just thinking about it! Any peppers will do, but the pointed, slightly smaller Ramiro peppers work particularly well because of their sweeter flesh. Once cooked, let this sit at room temperature for a short while so that all the lovely flavours meld together and the cheese marinates in the juices. Slices of toasted or wood-fired bread really set this off nicely.

4 small red or yellow peppers, sliced
1 fennel bulb, thinly sliced and fronds chopped
8 ripe tomatoes, halved
2 garlic cloves, thinly sliced
2 large red chillies, deseeded and thinly sliced
1 teaspoon sea salt
65 ml olive oil
200 g soft goats' cheese, sliced
a small handful of fresh basil leaves
2 tablespoons balsamic vinegar
toasted sourdough bread, to serve

Serves 4

Preheat the oven to 180°C (350°F) Gas 4. Put the peppers, fennel, fennel fronds, tomatoes, garlic and chillies in a large bowl with the salt and oil. Toss until evenly coated in the oil and arrange in a roasting tray. Roast in the preheated oven for about 1 hour, turning once after about 30 minutes, until the vegetables are just starting to char around the edges. Remove from the oven and let cool for 20–30 minutes

Lift the still-warm vegetables onto a large serving plate, reserving the cooking juices. Top with the cheese and basil leaves. Mix the reserved juices with the vinegar and spoon over the salad. Let sit for a little while before serving at room temperature, with toasted sourdough bread for mopping up the delicious juices.

tomato and mozzarella salad with aubergine relish

This aubergine relish takes its cue from the popular Sicilian side dish caponata – a combination of summer vegetables with olives and capers, gently spiked with wine vinegar. Left to cool, its bittersweet flavour intensifies and makes it the perfect partner for creamy buffalo mozzarella.

6 mixed ripe tomatoes, thinly sliced
3 large balls of fresh buffalo mozzarella, torn

aubergine relish:
1 medium aubergine, cut into small cubes
1 teaspoon salt
85 ml light olive oil
1 red onion, finely diced
2 garlic cloves, chopped
1 celery stick, finely diced
1 small red pepper, finely diced
1 tablespoon small salted capers, rinsed
90 g small black olives
65 ml red wine vinegar
2 teaspoons white sugar
a handful of fresh mint leaves, finely sliced
sea salt and freshly ground black pepper

Serves 4

To make the relish, put the aubergine in a colander with the salt and use your hands to toss together. Let sit for 30 minutes, then using your hands, squeeze out as much liquid from the aubergine as you can, without squashing the flesh too much.

Put the oil in a frying pan set over high heat. Add the onion and cook for 2 minutes. Add the aubergine and cook for 8–10 minutes, stirring often, until the aubergine turns golden. Add the garlic and cook for 1 minute only – don't let the garlic burn. Add the celery, red pepper, capers and olives and stir-fry for just 1 minute so that the vegetables stay crisp. Add the vinegar and sugar to the pan and bring to the boil, cooking for a minute. Remove from the heat and season to taste with salt and pepper. Let sit at room temperature for at least 30 minutes to allow the flavours to develop.

Arrange the tomato slices on a large serving plate and scatter the mozzarella pieces over the top. Spoon over the aubergine relish and sprinkle with the mint leaves to serve.

See photograph on page 94.

pasta primavera with lemony breadcrumbs

This light Italian pasta dish can be made using just about any crisp, green veggies you find at the spring farmers' markets, such as green beans, peas and young courgettes.

4 tablespoons light olive oil

100 g fresh white breadcrumbs

1 tablespoon finely grated zest from an unwaxed lemon

1 tablespoon fresh thyme leaves

50 g Parmesan cheese, finely grated

150 g peas (frozen or freshly shelled)

100 g green beans

1 bunch of baby asparagus, sliced

2 small courgettes, cut into batons

2 garlic cloves, chopped

2 ripe tomatoes, skinned, deseeded and chopped

400 g spaghetti or tagliatelle

sea salt and freshly ground black pepper

Serves 4

Put half of the oil in a frying pan set over medium heat. Add the breadcrumbs, lemon zest and thyme and cook for 4–5 minutes, stirring constantly, shaking the pan so that the breadcrumbs turn an even golden colour. Add 1 tablespoon of the Parmesan and stir until combined. Remove the mixture from the pan and set aside until needed.

Bring a large saucepan of lightly salted water to the boil and add the peas, beans, asparagus and courgettes. Cook for 2 minutes to just blanch and drain well. Heat the remaining oil in a large frying pan set over high heat, add the garlic and cook for just a few seconds to flavour the oil. Add the tomatoes and cook for 1 minute, until they are softened.

Return the blanched vegetables to the pan with the tomatoes, cook for 1–2 minutes and cover to keep warm. Cook the pasta according to the packet instructions. Drain well and return it to the warm pan. Add the vegetable and tomato mixture and half the lemony breadcrumbs and stir gently to combine. Season well with salt and pepper. Spoon onto serving plates and sprinkle with the remaining lemony breadcrumbs and Parmesan to serve.

See photograph on page 95.

peppery watercress and pea soup with Gorgonzola

Despite taking no time at all to prepare, there is something about watercress soup that seems quintessentially English and refined. Its mustardy bite sits nicely with the intensely flavoured Gorgonzola. Serve this as a starter when you want to make a good impression.

1 small bunch of watercress, about 300 g

50 g butter

1 onion, chopped

1 celery stick, chopped

100 g wild rocket leaves

½ teaspoon cracked black pepper

300 g peas (frozen or freshly shelled)

1.5 litres vegetable stock

100 g Gorgonzola cheese (optional)

Serves 4

Pick over the watercress to remove any discoloured leaves. Cut off and discard about 5 cm from the bottom of the stems. Roughly chop the leaves and remaining stems and set aside.

Put the butter in a large saucepan set over high heat and melt until sizzling. Add the onion and celery and cook for 2–3 minutes, until softened. Add the watercress, rocket and pepper and stir-fry for a couple of minutes until the greens wilt and start to pop in the hot pan. Add the peas and stock and bring to the boil. Reduce the heat and cook at a rapid simmer for 10 minutes, until all the vegetables are very soft. Transfer the mixture to a food processor or blender and whizz until smooth. Pass the mixture through a sieve into a clean saucepan and gently reheat.

Cut the Gorgonzola into 4 pieces (if using) and put 1 in the bottom of each of 4 warmed serving bowls. Ladle the hot soup over the top and serve immediately.

In Provençal dialect, pistou literally means 'pounded' and it's a highly appropriate name for this classic French sauce, which is made by crushing the ingredients in a mortar with a pestle. The resulting paste, similar in style to an Italian pesto, is then traditionally stirred into a rich vegetable soup to amplify its flavour. Just like a homemade pesto, pistou is best eaten as soon as possible, as it quickly becomes bitter. Try and find tender young broad beans for this light, broth-style soup – older beans will have tough skins and need to be shelled.

summer vegetable soup with pasta and pistou

2 tablespoons light olive oil
6 baby leeks, finely sliced
2 courgettes, cut into large dice
2 small yellow pattypan squash
1 small fennel bulb, cut into large dice
1 litre vegetable stock
100 g young pea pods
100 g fresh broad beans, shelled if necessary
50 g fresh pasta shape of your choice
freshly grated Parmesan cheese, to serve

pistou:
4 garlic cloves, chopped
½ teaspoon sea salt
2 tomatoes, skinned, deseeded and chopped
100 g fresh basil leaves, roughly torn
50 g fresh flat leaf parsley leaves
125 ml olive oil
2 tablespoons freshly squeezed lemon juice
25 g Parmesan cheese, finely grated

Serves 4

To make the pistou, put the garlic and salt in a large mortar and pound with a pestle until the garlic forms a smooth paste. Add the tomatoes and pound until smooth. Add the basil and parsley and pound until combined. Slowly add the olive oil until it is all incorporated. Add the lemon juice and Parmesan and stir to combine. Cover and refrigerate until needed.

Put the light olive oil in a large saucepan set over high heat. Add the leeks and cook for 2–3 minutes, stirring constantly. Add the courgettes, squash and fennel and cook, stirring, for 1–2 minutes until the vegetables soften but keep their colour. Add the stock and bring to the boil. Add the pea pods and broad beans and cook for 5 minutes. Add the pasta to the soup and gently simmer for 1–2 minutes, it is cooked but still retains a little 'bite'.

Ladle into warmed serving bowls, top with a dollop of pistou and sprinkle with Parmesan to serve.

Fresh chestnuts aren't always easy to find, but if you can get your hands on some, they really do make a wonderful addition to this pasta dish with a slightly festive flavour. Don't feel too guilty about the cream – the chestnuts are low in both fat and calories.

pappardelle pasta with portobello mushrooms, chestnuts and chives

200 g fresh chestnuts (optional)

1 tablespoon olive oil

15 g butter

2 garlic cloves, chopped

400 g portobello or field mushrooms, sliced

2 fresh thyme sprigs

125 ml dry white wine

250 ml single cream

1 bunch of chives, cut into 3-cm lengths

50 g Pecorino cheese, finely grated, plus extra to serve

400 g pappardelle, tagliatelle or any other ribbon pasta

sea salt and freshly ground black pepper

Serves 4

Preheat the oven to 200°C (400°F) Gas 6. Score a cross on one end of each chestnut. Put them on a baking tray and roast in the preheated oven for 10–15 minutes, until the skins split. Remove and let cool. When cool enough to handle, pull off the shells, and rub away the fleshy skin underneath. Set aside until needed.

Put the oil and butter in a frying pan set over high heat. When the butter sizzles, add the garlic and cook for just 1 minute, making sure it doesn't burn. Add the mushrooms and thyme, reduce the heat to medium and partially cover with a lid. Cook for 10 minutes, stirring often. Add the wine to the pan and simmer until the liquid is reduced by half. Add the cream, reduce the heat and cook for 15 minutes, until the mixture thickens. Add the chives and half of the Pecorino and stir to combine. Season to taste with salt and pepper. Cover with foil to keep warm.

Cook the pasta according to the packet instructions. Drain well and return to the warm pan. Add the mushroom sauce, gently toss to mix and serve immediately with extra Pecorino cheese for sprinkling.

root vegetable ragu with spiced couscous

This is a hearty dish packed with nutritious root veggies. My method for making couscous is not the traditional Moroccan way, but it does produce a full-flavoured version that makes the perfect accompaniment to the ragu.

3 tablespoons olive oil
25 g butter
1 red onion, chopped
1 celery stick, roughly chopped
6 garlic cloves, lightly smashed
500 ml passata
500 ml vegetable stock
2 tablespoons fresh oregano leaves
1 parsnip, peeled and chopped
2 carrots, peeled and chopped
6 small, waxy, new potatoes

spiced couscous:
375 ml vegetable stock
25 g butter
280 g medium grained couscous
1 teaspoon each of ground cumin, ground coriander and smoky Spanish paprika (pimentón)
¼ teaspoon cayenne pepper

Serves 4

Put the oil and butter in a large saucepan set over high heat. When the butter sizzles, add the onion, celery and garlic. Reduce heat to medium, partially cover the pan and cook for 10 minutes, stirring often, until the vegetables are soft and lightly browned. Add the passata, stock and oregano and bring to the boil. Reduce the heat to a medium simmer and cook, uncovered, for about 20 minutes. Add the parsnip, carrots and potatoes to the pan and cook for a further 15–20 minutes until tender.

To make the spiced couscous, put the stock and butter in a small saucepan set over high heat. Bring to the boil, then reduce the heat to low and keep the stock warm. Put the couscous and spices in a medium, heavy-based saucepan and cook over medium/high heat until the spices are aromatic and just start to turn a dusky brown. Turn off the heat. Pour the warm stock into the pan. Stir, cover with a tight-fitting lid and let sit for 10 minutes. Fluff up the couscous with a fork, cover again and let sit for a further 5 minutes. Tip the couscous out into a bowl and fluff up to separate as many grains as possible. Spoon onto serving plates, top with the root vegetable ragu and serve.

globe artichoke, tarragon and Roquefort soup

Artichokes can seem a little daunting, but in this recipe you don't have to worry about cutting out all of the fibrous, inedible bits – you just cook them until they are soft enough to remove. I'm always looking for ways to use tarragon, but it isn't easy, as its aromatic flavour can be a little overpowering. It works nicely here though, as does the Roquefort, making this a very special soup.

freshly squeezed juice of 1 lemon
8 large globe artichokes
1 tablespoon olive oil
25 g butter
1 large leek, sliced
1 garlic clove, chopped
2 tablespoons fresh tarragon leaves
500 ml vegetable stock
125 ml single cream
100 g Roquefort cheese, roughly crumbled
sea salt and freshly ground black pepper
Pumpkin and Caraway Seed Soda Bread (see page 36), to serve (optional)

Serves 4

Bring a large saucepan of water to the boil. Put the lemon juice and 1.5 litres water in a large bowl. Trim the leaves and stems from the artichokes. Cut each head in half and remove the hairy chokes. (Don't worry if you miss some of the gnarly bits, as they will come off more easily after cooking.) As you prepare each one, drop it in the bowl of water and lemon juice to prevent it from discolouring. When all the artichokes are prepared, add them to the pan of boiling water. Cook for 10–12 minutes and drain. Set aside. When cool enough to handle, trim the artichokes so that you are left with just the soft, fleshy bits.

Put the oil and butter in a large saucepan set over high heat. When the butter sizzles, add the leek and garlic, partially cover with a lid and cook for 5 minutes, until the leek sweats and softens. Add the tarragon and stir for 1 minute. Add the stock and bring to the boil. Add the artichokes and cook for 10 minutes. Transfer the mixture to a food processor or blender and whizz until smooth. Pour the mixture into a clean saucepan set over low heat and gently reheat. Add the cream, season to taste with salt and pepper and stir. Ladle the soup into warmed serving bowls, sprinkle with the Roquefort and serve with Pumpkin and Caraway Seed Soda Bread, if liked.

See photograph on page 104.

home-made cheese with roasted baby beetroot, fennel and pine nuts

Labneh is a Lebanese soft cheese – it's easy enough to make but you do have to prepare it a day in advance.

a bunch of baby beetroots (about 12), ends trimmed
100 g pine nuts
1 fennel bulb
1 tablespoon freshly squeezed lemon juice
2 garlic cloves, crushed
2 tablespoons olive oil
50 g mixed baby salad leaves
2 spring onions, thinly sliced
1 handful of fresh flat leaf parsley leaves
1 handful of fresh mint leaves

home-made cheese (labneh):
500 ml natural yoghurt, preferably sheeps'
1 teaspoon salt
3 tablespoons olive oil
4 small fresh lemon thyme sprigs

1 piece of muslin, about 30 cm square

Serves 4

Put the yoghurt and salt in a bowl and stir well. Line a sieve with the muslin, put the yoghurt into it, fold the muslin up over the top and set it over a bowl. Refrigerate for 36 hours. The yogurt will drain, leaving a firmer 'cheese-like' substance. You can help this process along by giving it a squeeze every few hours. Use 2 spoons to scoop out pieces and put them in a flat dish. Pour over the oil and add the lemon thyme. Cover and chill until needed.

Preheat the oven to 180°C (350°F) Gas 4. Put the beetroots in a roasting tin with 250 ml water and cover with foil. Roast in the preheated oven for 45 minutes, until easily pierced with a skewer. When cool enough to handle, peel off the skins and halve the beetroots. Put the pine nuts on a baking tray lined with baking paper and roast in the still-hot oven for 5 minutes, until just golden. Slice the fennel very thinly and put it in a bowl with half of the lemon juice. Put the garlic, oil and remaining lemon juice in a separate bowl and whisk to combine. Add the beetroot, salad leaves, spring onions and herbs to the bowl with the fennel, add the dressing and toss. Put the cheese on top and sprinkle with pine nuts to serve.

See photograph on page 105.

chilli and garlic steamed mushrooms with polenta

The flavours here are very Italian, but you could easily swap the parsley for coriander, add a splash of light soy sauce and suddenly find yourself in Asia. Almost any cultivated mushroom works here, but do try the recipe with fresh shiitake mushrooms if you decide to go the Asian route.

12 field mushrooms
65 ml dry white wine
65 ml olive oil
2 large red chillies, deseeded and chopped
2 garlic cloves, chopped
3 tablespoons finely chopped fresh flat leaf parsley

crisp polenta:
500 ml full-fat milk
150 g instant polenta
1 teaspoon sea salt
75 g butter
50 g Parmesan cheese, finely grated
250 ml light olive oil

a vegetable steamer, ideally bamboo

Serves 4

Cut any large stalks off the mushrooms and discard. Put the mushroom caps in a non-metallic, flat dish with the wine, oil, chillies and garlic and use your hands to toss the mushrooms around until coated with the marinade. Cover and let sit for 1 hour.

Sit the dish of mushrooms inside a large steamer, a large Asian bamboo steamer is ideal. Set the steamer over a large saucepan of boiling water, cover and steam for 20 minutes until tender.

Lightly oil a baking tray. Put the milk in a saucepan with 500 ml water and set over medium heat. Bring just to the boil, then pour the polenta into the saucepan in a steady stream, whisking constantly to avoid any lumps. Add the salt and stir for 5 minutes until the polenta is soft. Remove from the heat, add the butter and Parmesan and beat until the mixture is smooth. Spread the polenta out on the oiled baking tray and put in the refrigerator to chill. When completely cold, cut the polenta into 12 squares. Put the oil in a frying pan set over high heat, add the polenta slices and fry for 4–5 minutes on each side until golden and crisp. Remove them from the pan and drain any excess oil on kitchen paper. Put 3 slices of polenta onto each of 4 serving plates, spoon the mushrooms and juices over the top and sprinkle with the parsley to serve.

This is my vegetarian take on the classic Spanish rice dish paella. It's colourful, delicious and bursting with fresh, young vegetables grown on the vine and enhanced with the subtle flavour of saffron. Perfect for summer entertaining.

paella of summer vine vegetables with almonds

a large pinch of saffron threads

80 ml olive oil

200 g red or yellow cherry tomatoes

100 g green beans

4 baby courgettes, halved

80 g freshly shelled peas

2 garlic cloves, chopped

2 fresh rosemary sprigs

320 g Arborio risotto rice

800 ml vegetable stock

30 g flaked almonds, lightly toasted

Serves 4

Put the saffron in a bowl with 65 ml hot water and set aside to infuse. Heat half of the oil in a heavy-based frying pan set over high heat and add the tomatoes. Cook for 2 minutes, shaking the pan so that the tomatoes soften and start to split. Use a slotted spoon to remove the tomatoes from the pan and set aside. Add the beans, courgettes and peas and stir-fry over high heat for 2–3 minutes. Set aside with the tomatoes until needed.

Add the remaining oil to the pan with the garlic and rosemary and cook gently for 1 minute to flavour the oil. Add the rice to the pan and cook, stirring constantly, for 2 minutes, until the rice is shiny and opaque. Add the stock and saffron water to the pan. Stir just once or twice, then increase the heat and let the liquid reach the boil. When the stock is rapidly boiling and little holes have formed in the rice, reduce the heat to medium and let simmer gently for about 20 minutes, until almost all the stock has been absorbed.

Scatter the cooked tomatoes, beans, courgettes and peas over the rice, cover lightly with some foil and cook over low heat for 5 minutes so that the vegetables are just heated through. Sprinkle the almonds on top to serve.

The trick to this recipe is to take it slowly. I let the red pepper and chillies gently release their colour and flavour into the oil by roasting them in a low oven for a full hour. This is contemporary cooking at its best, as it draws on more than one style of cuisine, and it's very much my kind of Saturday night comfort food.

tagliatelle with pan-fried pumpkin and red pepper oil

1 tablespoon light olive oil

400 g pumpkin or winter squash, peeled, deseeded and chopped into 2–3 cm pieces

400 g pappardelle, tagliatelle or any other ribbon pasta

finely grated zest and juice of 1 unwaxed lemon

50 g wild rocket leaves

1 large handful of chopped fresh flat leaf parsley

sea salt and freshly ground black pepper

red pepper oil:

1 small red pepper, sliced

6 large red chillies, sliced

1 small red onion, sliced

4 garlic cloves, peeled but left whole

1 teaspoon cumin seeds

65 ml olive oil

Serves 4

Preheat the oven to 180°C (350°F) Gas 4. Put the red pepper, chillies, onion, garlic, cumin seeds and 2 tablespoons of the olive oil in a roasting tray. Cook in the preheated oven for 1 hour, turning often. Transfer the contents of the roasting tray to a food processor while still hot. Add the remaining oil and whizz until smooth. Let cool, then pour the mixture into a clean and dry screwtop jar.

Heat the light olive oil in a frying pan set over high and add the pumpkin. Cook for 10 minutes, turning often, until each piece is golden brown all over. Meanwhile, cook the pasta according to the packet instructions and drain well. Put it in a large bowl and add 2–3 tablespoons of the red pepper oil. Add the cooked pumpkin, lemon zest and juice, rocket and parsley and toss to combine. Season well with salt and pepper and serve immediately.

Note: The remaining red pepper oil will keep for 1 week when stored in an airtight jar in the fridge. It can be used as a dip for Crispy Oven Wedges (see page 22) or added to tomato-based sauces and soups for extra flavour.

Sometimes we forget how good the simple things can be. I was making a batch of vegetable stock (check out my recipe on page 65). It was early autumn, so I roasted the usual veggie suspects and threw in some whole garlic cloves and thyme sprigs. The tomatoes were overripe and juicy, and when combined with a splash of olive oil the resulting slow-roasted veggies were just too good to make a stock from. A few chickpeas were all that was needed to turn this unassuming tray of roasted vegetables into a great Saturday supper. I like to serve them with some Spicy Couscous (see page 103) to soak up the tasty juices.

roasted early autumn vegetables with chickpeas

12 small mushrooms

2 ripe tomatoes, halved

1 red pepper, cut into strips

1 yellow pepper, cut into strips

1 red onion, cut into wedges

1 small fennel bulb, sliced into thin wedges

1 garlic bulb, broken into individual cloves but left unpeeled

2 teaspoons sea salt

2 tablespoons olive oil

400-g tin chickpeas, drained and rinsed

2 fresh thyme or rosemary sprigs

Spiced Couscous (see page 103), to serve (optional)

Serves 4

Preheat the oven to 180°C (350°F) Gas 4. Put the mushrooms, tomatoes, red and yellow peppers, onion, fennel and garlic in a large roasting tray. Sprinkle the salt evenly over the vegetables and drizzle with the oil. Roast in the preheated oven for 1 hour.

Remove the tray from the oven and turn the vegetables. Add the chickpeas and thyme sprigs. Return the tray to the oven and roast for a further 30 minutes, until the edges of the vegetables are just starting to blacken and char.

To serve, spoon the Spiced Couscous (if using) onto serving plates and top with the warm roasted vegetables with chickpeas.

Stop press! This recipe was a last-minute addition to the book. Last summer was a hot one in Australia and I spent most of it outside experimenting on my new barbecue. The marinade here actually started out life as a dressing for a noodle salad from a recipe by the late American food writer Barbara Tropp (who was something of a genius when it came to contemporary Chinese cuisine). I really love it and was pleased to discover that it also works well as a marinade. You can use pretty much any combination of vegetables that you like, but remember to cook them separately, as it's best not to crowd the barbecue.

barbecued mixed vegetable platter

1 aubergine, cut into ½-cm thick slices
4 field mushrooms
1 bunch of thin asparagus spears
1 celery stick, cut into 3-cm lengths
1 red pepper, cut into 2-cm wide strips
vegetable oil, for brushing barbecue
steamed rice, to serve (optional)

soy balsamic marinade:
125 ml light soy sauce
65 ml balsamic vinegar
1 tablespoon olive oil
2 teaspoons white sugar

Serves 4

Put all of the ingredients for the marinade in a small bowl and whisk to combine. Arrange the vegetables in a large, non-metallic flat dish and pour over the marinade. Use your hands to toss the vegetables around in the marinade until evenly coated. Cover with clingfilm and let sit for 1 hour, turning often, to allow the flavours to develop.

Preheat the barbecue, hotplate or grill to high and brush lightly with vegetable oil. Use tongs to transfer the vegetables to a plate and reserve the marinade. Cook the aubergine and mushrooms first, for 2–3 minutes on each side, until dark brown, basting once or twice with a little of the reserved marinade. Transfer to a warmed serving plate. Put the asparagus, celery and red pepper on the barbecue and cook for 3–4 minutes on each side, basting with a little of the marinade as necessary. Transfer the vegetables to the serving plate with the aubergine and mushrooms.

Serve with steamed rice, if liked. Any remaining marinade can be poured into a jug and used as a sauce.

savoury baking

winter vegetable gratin

This is a great way to use up any combination of cold-weather root vegetables, especially those that are often overlooked like swede and my personal favourite parsnip.

200 g celeriac, peeled and cut into 3-cm pieces
1 carrot, peeled and cut into rounds
1 parsnip, peeled and cut into semi-circles
1 small swede, peeled and cut into chunks
2 potatoes, cut into 3–cm pieces
250 ml single cream
1 garlic clove, crushed
1 teaspoon mustard powder
50 g rye or brown breadcrumbs
2 tablespoons finely grated Parmesan cheese
2 teaspoons fresh marjoram leaves
25 g butter, melted
sea salt and freshly ground black pepper

Serves 6

Preheat the oven to 180°C (350°F) Gas 4 and lightly butter a medium ovenproof dish.

Bring a large saucepan of lightly salted water to the boil and add the celeriac, carrot, parsnip, swede and potatoes. Cook for 10 minutes, drain well and transfer the vegetables to a large bowl.

Put the cream, garlic and mustard powder in a small saucepan set over medium heat. Cook, stirring constantly, for about 10 minutes until the mixture is thick and coats the back of a spoon. Season to taste with salt and pepper and pour over the vegetables. Toss to combine and spoon the mixture into the buttered baking dish.

Put the breadcrumbs, Parmesan and marjoram in a bowl and mix together. Sprinkle the breadcrumbs over the vegetables and drizzle the melted butter over the top.

Cook in the preheated oven for about 40 minutes, until the breadcrumbs are golden and the mixture around the edge of the baking dish has formed a golden crust.

upside-down red pepper and tomato pie

It's a very Australian idea to have a tomato-and-onion based veggie fry-up and top it with a rustic dough that could easily be cooked over an open fire (but much easier done in an oven!) I have seen this done with mushrooms, but I think it really needs the juice of the tomatoes to lift it. This makes a great brunch dish for sharing.

2 tablespoons light olive oil
1 small red pepper, sliced
2 small red onions, quartered
2 garlic cloves, chopped
400-g tin chopped tomatoes
sea salt and freshly ground black pepper

pastry:
250 g plain flour
2 teaspoons baking powder
150 g Cheddar cheese, grated
1 teaspoon sea salt
50 g butter, melted
2 eggs, lightly beaten
65 ml buttermilk

Serves 6

To make the pastry, put the flour, baking powder, cheese and salt in the bowl of a food processor. Pulse a couple of times just to combine. Put the melted butter, eggs and buttermilk in a jug and whisk to combine. With the motor of the food processor running, slowly add the egg mixture until the dough becomes sticky. Let sit for 30 minutes while you make the topping.

Preheat the oven to 180°C (350°F) Gas 4. Put the oil in a large, non-stick frying pan with a heatproof handle and set over high heat. Add the red pepper, onions and garlic and cook for 10 minutes, until the pepper slices start to turn golden around the edges. Add the tomatoes, season well with salt and pepper and cook over high heat for 5 minutes, until almost all the liquid has evaporated from the pan. Leave the mixture in the pan and set aside to cool.

Tip the dough onto a lightly floured sheet of baking paper and form it into a rough circle about the same size as the frying pan. Carefully slide the dough onto the tomato mixture in the pan. Cook in the preheated oven for 20–25 minutes, until the pastry has risen and is light golden. Let cool for a few minutes before turning out onto a serving plate. Cut into slices and serve warm.

See photograph on page 120.

baked spinach mornay

This is really rich and ideally served with something doughy like the Upside-down Red Pepper and Tomato pie on page 119 or a simple green salad with a tangy vinaigrette. It is also a great brunch dish, perfect with poached eggs and hot buttered toast.

40 g butter

2 tablespoons plain flour

750 ml full-fat milk

200 g Fontina cheese, cubed

1 onion, chopped

1 garlic clove, chopped

1 kg fresh spinach leaves, chopped

¼ teaspoon freshly grated nutmeg

toasted and buttered sourdough bread, to serve (optional)

Serves 6

Preheat oven to 180°C (350°F) Gas 4. Put 25 g of the butter in a saucepan set over medium heat. When it is melted and sizzling, add the flour and cook for 1 minute, stirring constantly, until a thick paste forms.

Reduce the heat to low and slowly pour the milk into the pan, whisking constantly, until all the milk is incorporated and the mixture is smooth and lump-free. Add the cheese and stir until it has melted into the sauce. Set aside until needed.

Heat the remaining butter in a large frying pan set over high heat, add the onion and garlic and cook for 2–3 minutes, until the onion has softened. Add the spinach, cover with a lid, and cook for 4–5 minutes, stirring often, until the spinach has wilted. Transfer the spinach to a large bowl. Pour in the cheese sauce and stir to combine. Spoon the mixture into a large baking dish.

Sprinkle the nutmeg over the top and bake in the preheated oven for 30 minutes until the top of the mornay is golden and bubbling. Serve on slices of toasted and buttered sourdough bread, if liked.

See photograph on page 121.

herbed courgette and ricotta cheese tart

Filo pastry does have a tendency to become a bit soggy, but I have found that cooking this tart in a metal cake tin and sitting it on a preheated baking tray in the oven goes some way to solving the problem. This is particularly good served with the Greek Salad with Creamy Feta Dressing on page 90.

2 tablespoons olive oil

4–5 courgettes, grated

4 shallots, chopped

1 handful of finely shredded fresh basil leaves

1 handful of finely shredded fresh mint leaves

2 tablespoons finely chopped fresh dill

6 sheets of filo pastry, thawed if frozen

50 g butter, melted

200 g fresh ricotta cheese

3 eggs, lightly beaten

185 ml single cream

20-cm square, non-stick cake tin

Serves 6

Put the oil in a frying pan set over high heat. Add the courgettes and cook for 10 minutes, stirring often, until they start to brown. Transfer to a bowl and add the shallots and herbs. Stir to combine and set aside to cool.

Take a sheet of filo and lightly brush it all over with some of the melted butter. Fold it in half, brush the top lightly with butter and lay the filo in the cake tin, gently pressing it down onto the base and sides. Repeat with the remaining sheets of filo, stacking one on top of the other in the tin, until you have used them all. Cover with a clean, damp tea towel to keep the pastry moist.

Preheat the oven to 180°C (350°F) Gas 4 and put a baking tray on the centre shelf of the oven to heat. Put the ricotta, eggs and cream in a large bowl and add the courgette mixture. Stir well to combine, then spoon the mixture into the cake tin. Place the tin on the hot baking tray and bake in the preheated oven for about 30–35 minutes, until the filo is golden brown and crisp.

Let the tart cool for 10 minutes before cutting it into squares and serving warm or at room temperature.

I know it's tempting to buy ready-made pastry, but my recipe here is simplicity itself to make and tastes really good. You need not worry about shrinkage either, as leaving it untrimmed looks attractive in a rustic sort of way and ensures that it stays put.

red onion and goats' cheese quiche

75 g butter
4 red onions, thinly sliced
4 eggs, beaten
300 ml double cream
4 fresh thyme sprigs, roughly chopped
200 g soft goats' cheese
sea salt and freshly ground black pepper

shortcrust pastry:
185 g plain flour
125 g unsalted butter, cubed
1 teaspoon freshly squeezed lemon juice
2–3 tablespoons iced water

a 23-cm diameter ceramic flan dish

Serves 6–8

To make the pastry, put the flour and butter in the bowl of a food processor and put the bowl it in the freezer for 10 minutes. Remove it from the freezer and pulse the ingredients a few times only until they are just combined. With the motor of the food processor running, add the lemon juice and just enough iced water to allow the mixture to form a dough. Do not overbeat it, as this will make the pastry tough. Remove the dough and, using lightly floured hands, form it into a ball. Wrap the ball in clingfilm and let it rest in the fridge for 30 minutes.

Put the butter in a large saucepan set over high heat. When the butter is sizzling, add the onions and cook them, stirring constantly, for 1 minute. Reduce the heat to medium and gently cook for a further 20–25 minutes, stirring often, until the onions are soft and aromatic. Transfer the onions to a bowl and set aside to cool.

Preheat the oven to 180ºC (350ºF) Gas 4. Roll the pastry out on a sheet of lightly floured baking paper to form a circle about 30 cm in diameter. Use the paper to lift the pastry into the flan dish, gently pressing around the edges to seal. Prick the bottom and sides of the pastry with a fork. Cover the pastry with 2 layers of baking paper and top with uncooked rice or dried beans. Bake blind in the preheated oven for 15 minutes, until you can see the top of the pastry turning golden. Remove the paper and the rice or beans, brush the pastry case all over with a little of the beaten egg and return it to the oven for a further 5 minutes, until the bottom is dry and golden. Remove from the oven and set aside. Leave the oven on.

Put the eggs and cream in a bowl and season with salt and pepper. Spoon the onion mixture into the pastry case. Carefully pour in the egg mixture. Arrange the slices of goats' cheese over the top, scatter with the thyme sprigs and bake in the still-hot oven for about 30 minutes, until the quiche is lightly puffed up and golden. Let cool for 10 minutes before cutting into slices. Serve warm or at room temperature.

In my native Sydney, we are fortunate to have a plethora of excellent Turkish cafés and restaurants serving up fresh baked pide (Turkish bread) alongside colourful and delicious dips. The pide dough is also the base for the Turkish version of pizza, which is often filled or topped with the freshest of vegetables such as tomatoes, spinach or chard, or tangy feta cheese and sometimes with an egg or two cracked on top before being baked. It's very easy to see where the inspiration for this delicious pie came from!

Swiss chard, feta cheese and egg pie

3 tablespoons olive oil

2 garlic cloves, sliced

1 red onion, sliced

500 g Swiss chard, cut into 2-cm pieces

4 eggs

200 g feta cheese, crumbled

sea salt and freshly ground black pepper

pastry:

250 g plain flour

150 g unsalted butter, cubed

2 egg yolks

2–3 tablespoons iced water

Serves 6

To make the pastry, put the flour and butter in the bowl of a food processor and put the bowl in the freezer for 10 minutes. Pulse the ingredients a few times until just combined. With the motor of the food processor running, add the egg yolks and just enough iced water so that the mixture is on the verge of coming together. Do not overbeat, as this will make the pastry tough. Remove the dough from the bowl and use lightly floured hands to quickly form it into a ball. Wrap in clingfilm and let rest in the fridge for 30 minutes.

Put 2 tablespoons of the oil in a frying pan set over high heat, add the onion and garlic and cook for 2 minutes, until it softens and just flavours the oil. Add the Swiss chard to the pan and cook for about 5 minutes, stirring often, until it wilts and softens. Season well with salt and pepper, leave in the pan and set aside to cool.

Preheat the oven to 220ºC (425ºF) Gas 7. Roll the dough out on a sheet of lightly floured baking paper to form a circle about 35 cm in diameter, trimming away any uneven bits. Roll the edge over to form a 1-cm border, then roll over again. Transfer the pastry circle to a baking tray. Spoon the Swiss chard mixture over the pastry. Put the eggs in a bowl and prick the yolks with a fork. Pour the eggs over the Swiss chard so that they are evenly distributed, then scatter the feta over the top. Drizzle the remaining oil over the pie and cook in the preheated oven for about 20 minutes, until the pastry is golden and the top of the pie is just starting to turn brown.

Let cool for 10 minutes before cutting into slices to serve.

Lasagne may well be one of the best-loved of all Italian pasta dishes. Here, mushrooms are combined with Fontina and a creamy béchamel sauce, with mouthwatering results.

wild mushroom lasagne

50 g butter

1 tablespoon olive oil

1 large white onion, sliced

2 garlic cloves, chopped

2 bay leaves

1 kg wild mushrooms, sliced

250 ml vegetable stock

1 tablespoon tomato purée

375-g pack fresh lasagne sheets

300 g Fontina cheese, grated

50 g Parmesan cheese, finely grated

sea salt and freshly ground black pepper

béchamel sauce:

50 g butter

2 tablespoons plain flour

¼ teaspoon freshly grated nutmeg

750 ml full-fat milk

Serves 8

Put the butter in a saucepan set over medium heat. When the butter sizzles, stir in the flour and nutmeg and cook for 1 minute, stirring constantly. Remove from the heat and pour the milk into the pan, whisking constantly. Return the pan to low heat and cook for 5 minutes, stirring constantly, until the sauce is smooth and creamy.

Preheat the oven to 180°C (350°F) Gas 4. Put the butter and oil in a frying pan set over high heat and add the onion, garlic and bay leaves. Cook for 5 minutes until the onion has softened and turned opaque. Add the mushrooms, reduce the heat to medium and cook for 15 minutes, stirring occasionally, until the mushrooms are evenly cooked. Add the stock and tomato purée and increase the heat to high. Simmer rapidly until the liquid has reduced by half. Season well with salt and pepper.

Line the bottom of an oiled baking dish with lasagne sheets. Spread over a quarter of the sauce. Add one-third each of the mushrooms and grated cheese. Repeat the process and finish with a sheet of lasagne. Spoon over the remaining sauce and sprinkle with Parmesan. Bake in the preheated oven for 45 minutes, until golden brown and bubbling. Leave to rest for 10 minutes before serving.

Here are two of my favourite pizza toppings, but you can follow this basic pizza dough recipe and top it with whatever seasonal veggies and fresh herbs take your fancy.

two perfect pizzas

pizza dough:

15 g fresh yeast, crumbled

450 g strong white bread flour

1 teaspoon sea salt

2 tablespoons fine polenta

cherry tomato, courgette and mozzarella:

2 courgettes, thinly sliced

3 tablespoons olive oil

2 garlic cloves, crushed

200 g cherry tomatoes

1 large ball of fresh buffalo mozzarella, roughly torn

sea salt and freshly ground black pepper

potato and rosemary:

3 small, waxy, new potatoes, very thinly sliced, ideally using a mandoline

2 tablespoons olive oil

2 garlic cloves, chopped

2 tablespoons fresh rosemary needles

sea salt

Each pizza serves 4

To make the dough, put the yeast in a small bowl with 100 ml warm water. Stir to break up the yeast, then cover and let sit for 10 minutes, until the mixture looks bubbling and frothy. Put the flour and salt in a food processor and pulse a few times just to combine. Add another 100 ml warm water and the yeast mixture and process for a few seconds just to combine. Tip the dough out onto a lightly floured surface and knead it for 10 minutes. Oil the inside of a large bowl and sit the dough in it. Cover with a tea towel and let sit in a warm place until it has doubled in size. This will take about 1–1½ hours. Remove the dough from the bowl and punch it down. Divide in half. The dough can be wrapped in clingfilm and chilled for 3–4 hours before cooking or frozen to use another time.

Sprinkle the polenta on a work surface. Take each portion of dough and roll out to either a circle about 25 cm in diameter or a rectangle about 30 x 15 cm, as preferred. Make sure that the dough is less than ½ cm thick. Preheat the oven to 230°C (450°F) Gas 8.

To make the cherry tomato pizza, put the courgettes in a bowl with 2 tablespoons of the oil and the garlic. Season well with salt and pepper. Toss the courgettes around until evenly coated in the garlicky oil. Arrange the courgettes on the pizza base along with the cherry tomatoes. Sprinkle the mozzarella pieces over the top and drizzle with the remaining oil.

To make the potato pizza. Put the potato slices in a bowl with the oil and garlic and season well with salt. Arrange them on the pizza base, scatter with the rosemary needles and drizzle the garlicky oil from the bowl over the top.

Put 2 baking trays in the oven for 10–15 minutes, until they are very hot. Carefully transfer the pizzas to the trays and cook them in the preheated oven for about 20 minutes, until the dough around the edges turns golden. (If your oven is not big enough to take both pizzas side by side, you can cook them on 2 shelves, but do swap them over after 10 minutes of cooking.) Use a spatula to lift them up to check that the bases are cooked golden. Serve immediately.

Focaccia has long been a huge part of the café culture in my hometown of Sydney, where it is served toasted with all sorts of fillings. It's a rustic-style bread at its best, traditionally cooked over an open fire and made for tearing and sharing. If you like this recipe, try it again topped with other ingredients such as red onions, olives and sprigs of rosemary or thyme.

fennel and tomato focaccia

2 baby fennel bulbs, thinly sliced and fronds chopped
2 tomatoes, thinly sliced
1½ teaspoons sea salt flakes
extra virgin olive oil, to serve

focaccia dough:
450 g strong white bread flour
1 teaspoon salt
2 teaspoons dried yeast
3 tablespoons olive oil
plain flour, for kneading and dusting

Serves 6–8

For the dough, sift the flour and salt into a large bowl and add the yeast. Stir to combine and make a small well in the centre.

Add 300 ml warm water and 2 tablespoons of the olive oil. Quickly stir a few times just to combine, then use your hands to bring the mixture together. (If the mixture is sticking to your hands, add a little flour, but avoid using it if at all possible as adding too much during the kneading process can make the bread chewy.) Transfer the dough to a lightly floured surface and knead for 8–10 minutes, until smooth and elastic. Form the dough into a ball and put it in a lightly oiled bowl. Cover with a tea towel and let sit in a warm place for 1½ hours, until doubled in size.

Preheat the oven to 220°C (425°F) Gas 7. Put the ball of dough on a lightly oiled baking tray. Using a lightly floured rolling pin, gently roll from the centre upwards in one motion, not pressing too firmly so that any air bubbles stay intact. Roll from the centre down to the opposite end to form a rough oval shape, about 30 cm long and 20 cm at its widest point. Lightly cover and let sit again for 20–30 minutes until it has risen.

Use the tips of your fingers to press dimples over the surface of the dough. Lay the fennel and tomato slices on top and scatter with the fronds. Drizzle with the remaining olive oil and sprinkle with the salt flakes. Bake in the preheated oven for 25 minutes. Carefully slide the focaccia off of the tray and put it directly on the oven shelf. Cook for a further 5 minutes, until the crust is golden. Remove from the oven and let cool before eating. Serve with a small bowl of fruity extra virgin olive oil for dipping.

sweet things

Everyone needs a good chocolate cake recipe, and this could well be the one you've been waiting for! Each time I make this, the texture around the edge of the cake is just a little different to the time before, but it always has the same rich flavour with just a hint of tartness from the raspberries. For best results you will need to start making this the day before you want to eat it and chill overnight.

chocolate and raspberry mousse cake

200 g fresh raspberries

400 g dark cooking chocolate (no more than 70% cocoa solids), broken up

200 g unsalted butter, cubed

6 eggs, separated

30 g plain flour

55 g caster sugar

a 23-cm diameter springform cake tin, lightly greased or buttered

an ovenproof plate, large enough to sit on top of the cake tin, wrapped in foil

Serves 10–12

Put the raspberries on a tray lined with baking paper and put in the freezer for 2–3 hours. Preheat the oven to 200°C (400°F) Gas 6.

Put the chocolate and butter in a large, heatproof bowl and sit the bowl over a saucepan of gently simmering water. (Be careful not to let the bottom of the bowl come into contact with the hot water, as this will spoil the chocolate.) Slowly melt, stirring, until the mixture is smooth and silky, then remove from the heat.

Beat the egg yolks with the flour for 1 minute until thick, making sure there are no lumps. Add to the chocolate mixture and stir well to combine. In a separate, grease-free bowl, beat the egg whites with an electric whisk until they form soft peaks. Sprinkle the sugar over the whites and beat until you have a glossy shine. Use a large metal spoon to fold the egg whites into the chocolate and flour mixture. Do this in 2 batches, working quickly and without overbeating. Add the frozen berries and stir.

Pour the mixture into the cake tin and bake in the preheated oven for 15 minutes. Open the oven, leaving the heat on, and gently sit the foil-wrapped plate on top of the cake tin. Bake for a further 10 minutes. Carefully remove the cake tin from the oven, leaving the plate on top, and let cool completely. When cool, put the cake in the fridge and leave overnight. Remove from the fridge 3 hours before serving so that it comes to room temperature.

Crumbles are normally considered to be a comforting winter pudding, but this deliciously light, nutty version makes the most of juicy summer nectarines. It takes very little time to prepare and tastes sublime with ice cream.

nectarine and pistachio summer crumble

70 g whole pistachio nuts, coarsely chopped

50 g blanched whole almonds

60 g ground oatmeal

50 g cold unsalted butter, cubed

60 g plain flour

50 g soft brown sugar

6 nectarines

vanilla ice cream or double cream, to serve

Serves 6

To make the crumble topping, put the pistachios and almonds in a food processor and process until coarsely chopped. Transfer to a bowl. Add the oatmeal and butter and use your fingertips to rub the ingredients together until the mixture resembles coarse, wet sand. Add the flour and sugar and rub together to combine. Cover and refrigerate until needed.

Preheat the oven to 220°C (425°F) Gas 7. Line a baking tray with baking paper. Cut the nectarines in half. If the stone does not come out easily, don't worry – simply slice the flesh off the fruit and drop it directly onto the baking tray. Sprinkle the crumble topping evenly over the nectarines and bake in the preheated oven for 10–15 minutes, until the fruit is soft and juicy and the topping is a soft golden colour. Serve warm with ice cream or double cream.

Next time: This crumble works well with any stone fruits so try it with peaches, apricots or plums.

These are very pretty desserts, perfect for entertaining, as they can be made well in advance and popped in the fridge until you are ready to serve. Note that early forced rhubarb is more tender and will cook much more quickly than the later, ruby-coloured stalks. Keep your eye on it as it cooks. You don't want a pink mush, but rather a softly poached fruit that's still intact. I like my custard silky smooth, but if you prefer a thicker custard, simply cook it for a bit longer, until it coats the back of a wooden spoon.

rhubarb and custard pots

600 g rhubarb, chopped into 3-cm lengths
3 tablespoons caster sugar
1 teaspoon finely grated orange zest
2 tablespoons freshly squeezed orange juice

custard:
250 ml single cream
250 ml double cream
1 vanilla pod, split in half lengthways
4 egg yolks
2 tablespoons caster sugar
2 tablespoons toasted flaked almonds

6 individual serving dishes

Serves 6

Put the rhubarb, sugar, orange zest and juice in a saucepan with 2 tablespoons water and set over high heat. Cook, stirring constantly, until the mixture boils. Reduce the heat to medium and simmer for 5 minutes, until the rhubarb is soft but still retains some shape. Spoon the rhubarb into the serving dishes and set aside to cool while you make the custard.

Put both the single and double cream in a saucepan. Set over low heat and add the vanilla pod. Slowly bring the cream to the boil. As the cream boils, remove the pod and scrape the seeds into the custard, discarding the bean. Put the egg yolks and sugar in a bowl and whisk for 1 minute. Slowly pour the hot cream into the yolk mixture, whisking constantly. Transfer the mixture to a clean saucepan and set over low heat. Cook for 5 minutes, being careful not to let it boil.

While still warm, spoon the custard over the rhubarb and let the pots cool in the fridge for at least 3 hours or overnight.

pear and ginger crumble cake

This is a deliciously spicy cake with a very moreish texture. Note that ground ginger loses its intensity if left sitting in the storecupboard for too long, so do make sure that what you use here is not past it's use-by date. I have made this recipe many times substituting apples for the pears. If you decide to try it, use ground cinnamon instead of the ginger.

125 g unsalted butter, softened
125 g caster sugar
2 eggs, at room temperature
125 g plain flour
2 teaspoons baking powder
2 firm pears, peeled, cored and sliced
1 tablespoon freshly squeezed lemon juice
double cream, to serve (optional)

ginger crumble:
60 g plain flour
1 teaspoon ground ginger
3 tablespoons soft light brown sugar
50 g cold unsalted butter, cubed

a 20-cm diameter springform cake tin, base-lined with baking paper and lightly greased

To make the crumble mixture, put the flour and ginger in a large bowl. Add the cold butter and quickly rub it into the flour using your fingertips. Add the sugar and rub again until the mixture resembles coarse sand. Refrigerate until needed.

Preheat the oven to 180°C (350°F) Gas 4. Beat the softened butter and sugar with an electric whisk until pale and creamy. Add the eggs, 1 at a time, and beat well between each addition. Tip in the flour and baking powder and beat for 1 minute, until the mixture is smooth and well combined. Pour it into the prepared cake tin. Toss the pears in a bowl with the lemon juice and put them on top of the cake. Sprinkle the crumble topping over the top and bake in the preheated oven for 40–45 minutes, until the cake is golden on top.

Let cool slightly before removing from the tin and serving warm with double cream, if liked.

upside-down peach cake

You can use either yellow or white peaches here. I prefer the more robust flavour of yellow peaches – the white ones have a more subtle flavour that is more like that of nectarines, which are, after all, peaches without the fuzzy skin. Look out for locally grown, market-fresh, juicy summer peaches and try to resist eating them before you make this delicious cake!

4 large peaches
125 g unsalted butter, softened
185 g soft brown sugar
3 eggs, separated
185 g self-raising flour
250 g sour cream
icing sugar, for dusting
single cream, to serve (optional)

a 23-cm diameter springform cake tin, base-lined with baking paper and lightly greased

Preheat the oven to 180°C (350°F) Gas 4. Halve the peaches, discard the stone, then cut each half in half again. Arrange the peach quarters on the bottom of the cake tin and set aside while making the cake mixture.

Put the butter and sugar in a large bowl and beat with an electric whisk until the sugar has completely dissolved and the mixture is the colour of caramel. Add the egg yolks, 1 at a time, beating for 1 minute between each addition. Fold the flour and sour cream through in 2 batches.

In a separate grease-free bowl, beat the egg whites with an electric whisk until they form firm peaks. Using a large metal spoon, fold the whites into the cake mixture in 2 batches. Spoon the mixture over the peaches and bake in the preheated oven for 40–45 minutes, until the top of the cake is golden and the centre springs back when gently pressed.

Let cool for 10 minutes before carefully turning out onto a serving plate. Dust with icing sugar and serve warm with single cream for pouring, if liked.

See photograph on page 144.

almond and lemon cake

Lemons and almonds are a flavour match made in heaven. It is all too easy to buy almonds pre-ground in packets, but by the time they reach you they have lost much of their flavour. Grinding your own only takes a few minutes and the almond oil in the nuts is slowly released as the cake bakes in the hot oven to give a full and rich flavour. This cake is delicious eaten warm from the oven for afternoon tea or served with some vanilla ice cream as a dessert.

250 g blanched whole almonds
3 unwaxed lemons
200 g butter
200 g caster sugar
3 eggs
75 g plain flour
1 teaspoon baking powder

lemon icing:
150 g icing sugar
2 tablespoons freshly squeezed lemon juice

a 20-cm square cake tin, base-lined with baking paper and lightly greased

Serves 8–10

Preheat the oven to 180°C (350°F) Gas 4.

Put the almonds on a baking tray and toast in the preheated oven for 5 minutes, until aromatic and just starting to turn golden. Let cool, then transfer to a food processor. Process the nuts until finely chopped and set aside until needed.

Finely grate the zest from 2 of the lemons and squeeze all 3 of them so that you have 80 ml lemon juice. Put the butter, caster sugar and lemon zest in a bowl and, using an electric whisk, beat for about 5 minutes, until the mixture is thick. Add the eggs, 1 at a time, and beat well between each addition. Fold in the flour, baking powder and ground almonds. Add the lemon juice and stir to combine. Spoon the mixture into the prepared tin and bake in the preheated oven for about 35 minutes, until the top of the cake is golden and the centre springs back when gently pressed. Remove from the tin and let cool.

To make the icing, beat the icing sugar with the lemon juice for 2 minutes. Drizzle the icing over the cake and let set before serving.

See photograph on page 145.

carrot and walnut cake with cream cheese filling

Carrot cake began its life as a hippy cake in the 70s and was then mass produced for the booming Sydney café scene in the 80s. My version is crumbly and soft and probably best eaten with a spoon. If you are nervous about cutting the cake through the centre, simply spread the filling over the top of the cooled cake instead.

2 eggs, separated
110 g raw (unrefined) sugar
200 ml light olive oil
1 teaspoon bicarbonate of soda
185 g plain flour
2 teaspoons baking powder
1 teaspoon ground cinnamon
¼ teaspoon freshly grated nutmeg
200 g grated carrot
100 g walnut halves

cream cheese filling:
250 g cream cheese
125 g butter, cubed
3 tablespoons brown sugar
2–3 tablespoons maple syrup

an 18-cm diameter springform cake tin, lightly greased

Serves 8

Preheat the oven to 180°C (350°F) Gas 4.

Put the egg yolks and raw sugar in a large bowl and beat for 2 minutes. Add the oil and bicarbonate of soda and beat until just combined. Fold in the flour, spices, carrot and walnuts until combined. The mixture should look quite thick. In a separate grease-free bowl, beat the egg whites with an electric whisk until they form soft peaks then fold them into the cake mixture in 2 batches. Spoon the cake mixture into the cake tin and bake for 45–50 minutes, until golden and slightly puffed. Let the cake cool in the tin for about 10 minutes before turning it out onto a wire rack.

To make the filling, put the cream cheese and butter in a bowl and let them come to room temperature. Add the brown sugar and, using an electric whisk, beat for 5 minutes, until there are no lumps and the beaters leave a trail when turned off. Add the maple syrup a little at a time and beat for a further 2 minutes, until the mixture is smooth and a spreadable consistency. Carefully slice the cooled cake in half and spread the filling on the bottom layer.

cherry and ricotta strudel

This fruit-filled strudel is, like the carrot cake on page 146, just a little bit retro, but I think some things do enough time in culinary purgatory to warrant a comeback! Fresh ricotta cheese is combined with summer-ripe cherries and crispy filo with great success. Best of all, you can make this in advance and freeze it. There is no need to thaw before cooking – just give it a little more time in the oven. You could try using sliced green apples instead of the cherries.

500 g fresh cherries, stoned
60 g icing sugar, plus extra for dusting
2 teaspoons cornflour
8 sheets of filo pastry, thawed if frozen
100 g ground almonds (pre-packaged or see Almond and Lemon Cake on page 146)
150 g fresh ricotta cheese
75 g unsalted butter, melted

Serves 8

Put the cherries, 1 tablespoon of the icing sugar and the cornflour in a bowl and let sit for 30 minutes, stirring often. Preheat the oven to 220°C (425°F) Gas 7.

Put the ground almonds and 2 tablepoons of the remaining icing sugar in a bowl and mix to combine. Put the ricotta in a separate bowl, add the remaining icing sugar and mix to combine. Set aside until needed. Put a baking tray in the preheated oven to heat up. (This will prevent the bottom of the filo becoming soggy.)

Put a sheet of baking paper on a work surface. Lay a sheet of filo on the baking paper, longest edge nearest to you. Brush all over with melted butter until the filo is shiny. Sprinkle 1–2 tablespoons of the ground almond mixture over the pastry. Repeat with the remaining sheets of filo, butter and almond mixture, finishing with the final sheet of filo.

Working quickly, so that the filo does not become soggy, spread the ricotta mixture over the pastry, leaving a 5-cm margin around the edges. Spoon the cherry mixture over the top. Fold the edge nearest to you up and over the filling, tucking in the shorter edges as you roll. Make sure the strudel is sitting seam-side down. Use the baking paper to lift the strudel onto the hot baking tray. Bake in the preheated oven for 12–15 minutes, until lightly golden brown.

Remove and let cool slightly before dusting liberally with icing sugar and cutting into slices to serve.

fresh fig and walnut meringue

Maggie Beer is a popular character in the Australian food scene and she is a passionate advocate of farm-fresh produce. The inspiration for this meringue comes from one of her recipes, but she uses dried figs rather than fresh. Don't use big figs here, as they will split and prevent the egg whites from cooking and the meringue will become sloppy. I found some small, very black ones that were perfect with the caramelly meringue.

150 g walnut halves
8–10 small black fresh figs, halved
6 large egg whites
230 g soft light brown sugar

a 23-cm diameter circle of baking paper

Serves 8–10

Preheat the oven to 180°C (350°F) Gas 4. Put the walnuts on a baking tray and toast in the preheated oven for 5 minutes, until just starting to turn golden. Remove and let cool. Leave the oven on.

Put the egg whites in a large, grease-free bowl and beat with an electric whisk until they form soft peaks. Add a tablespoon of the sugar at a time, beating well between each addition, and continue until all the sugar has been added and the meringue resembles a thick, fluffy caramel. Add the figs and walnuts and stir to combine.

Put the circle of baking paper on a baking tray. Use a large spoon to transfer the mixture onto the paper, keeping within the circle and using the back of the spoon to create dents and peaks for a rustic effect. Bake in the preheated oven for 40–45 minutes, until the peaks of the meringue are a dark golden colour.

Allow to cool for 15 minutes then slide a large knife under the meringue to remove it from the paper and transfer it to a serving plate. This is best eaten warm or a room temperature.

See photograph on page 150.

strawberry meringue roulade

I love meringues, but I am not too fond of the pressure to make the conventional 'perfect' meringue. I'm all for messy recipes – those that you actually want to eat, not those that you're afraid to touch! It doesn't matter if this meringue splits or isn't crispy; it's not meant to be. It's really just an excuse to eat lots of fresh strawberries and cream. Simple.

3 egg whites
1 teaspoon cornflour
170 g caster sugar, plus 2 teaspoons
125 ml whipping cream
3 tablespoons icing sugar, plus extra for dusting
250 g fresh strawberries, hulled and sliced

Serves 4–6

Preheat the oven to 130°C (250°F) Gas ½. Line a baking tray with baking paper and sprinkle over 1 teaspoon caster sugar. (This will stop the meringue from sticking.)

Put the egg whites in a grease-free bowl, add the cornflour and beat with an electric whisk until soft peaks form. Add 1 tablespoon of sugar at a time, beating well between each addition, and continue beating until you can no longer feel grains of sugar when you rub the mixture between your thumb and forefinger. Use a large metal spoon to transfer the mixture to the prepared baking tray and smooth it out with a palette knife. You want a rectangle about 20 x 30 cm and no thicker than 1 cm. Bake the meringue in the preheated oven for 20 minutes, until it is just set and the top turns a light caramel colour and is no longer sticky when lightly touched.

Take a second piece of baking paper, slightly larger than the meringue, and sprinkle over 1 teaspoon caster sugar. Quickly flip the tray upside-down so that the meringue is turned out onto the paper. Tap the bottom of the tray so that the meringue comes away in one piece. Peel off the bottom piece of baking paper. Firmly roll the meringue up into a log with the second sheet of paper and wrap in a clean tea towel. Set aside to cool completely.

Put the cream and icing sugar in a bowl and whisk until firm peaks form. Unroll the meringue. Spoon the cream over the meringue, leaving a 2-cm margin around the edge. Arrange the sliced strawberries over the cream and roll up. Dust liberally with icing sugar and cut into thick slices to serve.

See photograph on page 151.

coconut creamed rice with poached plums

Tinned coconut milk is a must-have pantry staple for me, as I use it in lots of dishes, both savoury and sweet. This is a particular favourite. At the market, choose a sweet, large variety of plum for poaching and pick fruits with a silvery patina, as it's an indicator of freshness. The coconut creamed rice is also lovely with poached cherries.

8 plums, halved and stoned
115 g raw (unrefined) sugar
1 cinnamon stick
2 green cardamom pods

creamed coconut rice:
100 g short-grain rice
2 x 400-ml tins coconut milk
115 g white or caster sugar
125 ml whipping cream

Serves 6

To make the coconut creamed rice, put the rice in a sieve and rinse it under cold running water until the water runs clear. Drain well. Put the rice in a large saucepan set over high heat and add the coconut milk and sugar. Bring to a gentle boil, then reduce the heat to low and cook for 25–30 minutes, stirring often to ensure that the rice doesn't catch. Let cool. Whip the cream until soft peaks form, then fold it into the rice mixture.

Meanwhile, put the plums, sugar, cinnamon stick and cardamom pods in a saucepan and add 250 ml water. Bring to the boil, then reduce heat to low and cook for 20 minutes, gently turning the plums often, until they soften but retain their shape. Remove the cinnamon stick and cardamom pods from the pan.

Divide the creamed rice between serving dishes and spoon the warm plums over the top. Serve immediately.

Granny Smith apples were first cultivated in my hometown of Sydney by Maria Ann Smith (aka granny!) I suppose she saw their potential as a good all-round cooking apple. Their flesh collapses when cooked, making them perfect for apple sauce. I like them in sweet puddings, such as this self-saucing one, but they are not ideal for tarts and cakes. I've used mild, sweet blueberries here as they are widely available, but if you find mulberries (truly seasonal and rarely grown commercially), don't hesitate to use them in this pudding.

baked Granny Smith and blueberry pudding

2 tart green apples, such as Granny Smith

150 g blueberries

125 g plain flour

3 teaspoons baking powder

115 g caster sugar

250 ml buttermilk

1 egg

1 vanilla pod

100 g soft light brown sugar

single cream, to serve (optional)

Serves 6

Preheat the oven to 180ºC (350ºF) Gas 4 and generously butter a medium baking dish. Peel and core the apples then thinly slice them directly into the baking dish, arranging them in the bottom of the dish with the blueberries.

Sift the flour, baking powder and caster sugar into a large bowl. Put the buttermilk and egg in a separate bowl. Split the vanilla pod in half lengthways and scrape the seeds from the pod directly into this bowl, then stir to combine. Pour the buttermilk mixture into the flour mixture and beat well to combine.

Pour the mixture over the fruit in the baking dish. Working quickly, put the brown sugar in a jug and add 250 ml boiling water. Stir until the sugar has dissolved. Carefully pour this mixture into the baking dish, pouring into a corner. Bake the pudding in the preheated oven for 45 minutes, until the surface feels dry and springs back when lightly touched. Serve warm with cream for pouring, if liked.

This is an impressive pudding for relatively little work. The sweet and buttery brioche works well with the tangy blackberries. Try and buy very sweet blackberries for this, as they will be softer and juicier, which is exactly what you want here. The dark purple juices should bleed into the pudding to create a pretty, marbled effect.

baked brioche pudding with blackberries

4 brioche rolls or ½ 400-g brioche loaf

50 g butter, softened

300 g fresh blackberries

3 eggs

125 ml single cream

375 ml full-fat milk

75 g caster sugar

2 tablespoons raw (unrefined) sugar

vanilla ice cream, to serve (optional)

Serves 6

Slice the brioche to give you 6–8 thin slices. Lightly butter the slices on one side and arrange them in the bottom of a medium baking dish, overlapping them slightly. Put half the blackberries on top. Repeat with the remaining brioche slices and blackberries. Put the cream, eggs, milk and caster sugar in a bowl or jug and beat to combine. Pour the mixture over the brioche in the baking dish. Cover with foil and let sit for 30 minutes to allow the brioche to absorb the liquid.

Preheat the oven to 180ºC (350ºF) Gas 4. Sprinkle the raw sugar over the top of the pudding and bake it in the preheated oven for 40–45 minutes, until the top of the pudding is golden brown. Serve warm with vanilla ice cream, if liked.

websites and mail order

where to buy seasonal food

www.farmersmarkets.net
The National Association of
Farmers' Markets
*Provides an up-to-date listing of farmers'
markets throughout the UK.*

www.farmshopping.com
Farm Retail Association
*A comprehensive listing of farms
throughout Britain that sell their
produce direct.*

www.bigbarn.co.uk
*Search for farmers' markets, vegetable
delivery box schemes and suppliers within
a 5–50 mile radius of your own postcode.*

www.thefoody.com
*Search for farmers' markets in your area
and see an up-to-date food events diary
for the UK.*

home delivery and mail order

Abel & Cole
*Organic fruit and vegetable delivery
throughout the UK, with a focus on British
seasonal produce.*
www.abel-cole.co.uk

Riverford Organic Vegetables
*Vegetables delivered in the south of
England and Wales.*
www.riverford.co.uk

www.natoora.co.uk
*An online farmers' market. Fresh fruit,
vegetables, cheeses and deli foods all
available to order online for home delivery
within the UK.*

The Herb Farm
*Marvellous selection of live herb plants
delivered to your door, including numerous
varieties of oregano and rosemary.*
www.theherbfarm.co.uk

Seeds of Italy
*Real Italian seeds supplied mail order for
growing your own Italian fruit, vegetables
and herbs. They offer 5 types of basil and
over 20 varieties of tomato.*
www.seedsofitaly.com

Neal's Yard Dairy
*Shops and restaurants across the UK plus
mail order of fine cheeses.*
www.nealsyarddairy.co.uk

Food markets

www.boroughmarket.org.uk
*London's oldest food market is a busy
wholesale fruit and vegetable market and
major tourist attraction.*

www.country-markets.co.uk
WI Country Markets
*A guide to the many Women's Institute
markets around the UK.*

cookery tours and classes

www.celiabrooksbrown.com
*Popular gastro tours in Borough and
Portobello Road markets in London. Tour
guide is Celia Brooks Brown, a leading
vegetarian food writer and consultant.*

www.booksforcooks.com
*Notting Hill's famous cookbook shop
runs a programme of cookery workshops.
Recent classes have included vegetarian
Lebanese and Thai food. See website for
further details.*

www.fabfoodtrails.com
*One-, two- and three-day trips around
Ireland, meeting food producers and
sampling the finest Irish produce.*

www.discoverthetaste.com
*Gastro tours based in Edinburgh offering
walks around the city, via farmers' markets
and delis, plus cooking demonstrations
and courses.*

interesting food-related organizations

The Vegetarian Society
*The Vegetarian Society is a registered
charity supported by its members. It is
dedicated to education and to that end
has its own vegetarian cookery school
'Le Cordon Vert'. See website for details.*
www.vegsoc.org

www.veggieplaces.co.uk
*An information portal, providing a useful
service by identifying places across the UK
that cater well for vegetarians through
information and reviews from visitors.*

The Soil Association
*A campaigning group for organic farming
with a wealth of information about food
and farming methods.*
www.soilassociation.org

Common Ground
*A charity that champions local diversity;
its websites offer a lot of information about
local events and traditions, many relating
to organic food.*
www.commonground.org.uk

www.food.gov.uk
*Independent watchdog established to
protect the public's health and consumer
interests in relation to food safety and
standards. Features up-to-date information
on labelling guidelines for vegetarian and
vegan products.*

index

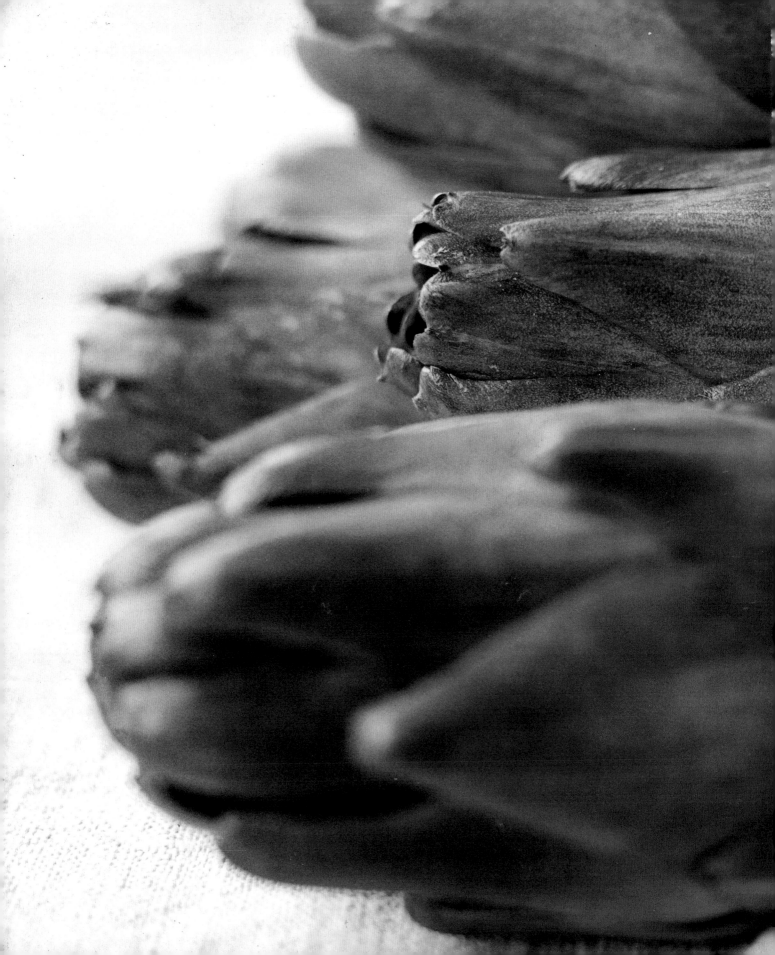